ST. NIKEPHOROS OF CHIOS

Ἀπολυτίκιον. Ἦχος δ΄. Ὁ ἔνσαρκος Ἄγγελος.

Ἀστὴρ φαεινότατος τῆς Ἐκκλησίας Χριστοῦ, λιμὼν δαψιλέστατος τῆς ἀληθείας αὐτοῦ καὶ σάλπιγξ μελίρρυτος, δέδειξαι Νικηφόρε, οὐρανόθεν τοῖς θείοις, νάμασι καθηδύνων τῶν πιστῶν τὰς καρδίας. Δι᾽ ὃ πρέσβευε Χριστῷ τῷ Θεῷ, σωθῆναι τὰς ψυχὰς ἡμῶν.

Κοντάκιον. Ἦχος δ΄. Ἡ Παρθένος σήμερον.

Νικηφόρον σήμερον ἡ Χίος πᾶσα γεραίρει, τὸν σταυρὸν ἀράμενον τοῦ Ἰησοῦ θαρσαλέως, ἕλκοντα πρὸς σωτηρίαν τοὺς ὀρθοδόξους, ᾄδοντα μετὰ δικαίων καὶ τῶν ὁσίων, ἐν ᾠδαῖς, ἄσμασιν, ὕμνοις, δόξαν προσφέρειν τῷ ἐν ὑψίστοις Θεῷ.

Μεγαλυνάριον.

Τὸν ἐν ἱερεῦσι καὶ μοναστᾶῖς καὶ ἐν διδασκάλοις, ὑμνογράφοις καὶ τοῖς σοφοῖς, τὸν βλαστὸν τῆς Χίου Νέας Μονῆς τὸ κλέος, τὸν θεῖον Νικηφόρον, ὕμνοις τιμήσωμεν.

Apolytikion

Thou hast been shown to be, O Nikephoros, a most luminous star of the Church of Christ, an exceedingly rich meadow of His truth, and a mellifluent clarion, delighting the hearts of the faithful with divinely inspired teachings. Wherefore intercede with Christ God for the salvation of our souls.

Kontakion

Today all of Chios honoreth Nikephoros who did take up the cross of Jesus courageously, drawing the Orthodox towards salvation, chanting with the righteous and the holy ascetics odes, songs and hymns, to offer glory to God in the highest.

Megalynarion

Let us honor with hymns the divine Nikephoros, the offspring of Chios and glory of the Monastery of Nea Moni, who did shine among priests, monastics and teachers, hymnographers and the wise.

Ὁ ἅγιος Νικηφόρος ὁ Χίος

ST. NIKEPHOROS OF CHIOS

MODERN ORTHODOX SAINTS

4

ST. NIKEPHOROS OF CHIOS

Outstanding Writer of Liturgical Poetry and Lives of Saints, Educator, Spiritual Striver, and Trainer of Martyrs. An account of his Life, Character and Message, together with a Comprehensive List of his Publications, Selections from them, and Brief Biographies of eleven Neomartyrs and other Orthodox Saints who are treated in his works

By

CONSTANTINE CAVARNOS

INSTITUTE FOR BYZANTINE
AND MODERN GREEK STUDIES
115 Gilbert Road
Belmont, Massachusetts 02178
U.S.A.

PREFACE

St. Macarios of Corinth (1731-1805), to whom volume 2 of the series *Modern Orthodox Saints* is devoted, was a mentor of two learned saints: Nicodemos the Hagiorite (1749-1809) and Nikephoros of Chios (1750-1821). Having dealt in volume 3 with St. Nicodemos, who was born about a year earlier than St. Nikephoros and was outlived by the latter, I have thought it quite appropriate to devote volume 4 to St. Nikephoros.

This is the first book on St. Nikephoros to appear in English. It serves not only to make better known his life, character, work and thought, but also to shed further light on St. Macarios of Corinth, who is often referred to in its pages. Macarios settled in 1790 as a hermit in Chios. And from that time until the repose of Macarios in 1805, the two saints were in frequent association with one another.

The "Introductory" is a somewhat expanded and revised version of a lecture which I delivered at Hellenic College, Boston, on November 20, 1974, under the sponsorship of the Byzantine Fellowship. It appears in print for the first time. The second chapter, containing "The Life of St. Nikephoros by Emily Sarou," daughter of the eminent Chian historiographer and educator George I. Zolotas, was first published in 1907 in Chios. I have translated it from the original Greek and annotated it. The "Works of the Saint," which follows, is the first comprehensive list to be published. "Selected Passages from the Prose Works of the Saint," and "Anthology from the Poetry of the Saint," which come next, have been compiled with a view to giving some of the most representative, instructive, and uplifting selections from his writings. Finally, the Appendix of "Brief Biographies" was written to provide helpful information about eleven modern martyrs and eight other Orthodox saints who are treated in St. Nikephoros' works and are mentioned in this book.

I owe many thanks to the Most Reverend Chrysostomos Gialouris, Metropolitan of Chios, for promptly responding to my request for photocopies of certain of the writings of St. Nikephoros, and for a photograph of his old icon which is in the Church of Hypapanti at Upper Kardamyla, Chios. The photograph has been used as the model for the frontispiece of this volume. I am also very grateful to Father Gregory of Holy Transfiguration Monastery in Boston for drawing the frontispiece; to Father Ephraim of the same monastery for reading the anthology from the poetry and suggesting a good number of improvements in expression; and to Dr. John Johnstone, Jr., for reading the entire manuscript and making many valuable comments.

CONTENTS

St. Nikephoros of Chios

Panel icon. Ca. 1907. Church of Hypapanti,
Upper Kardamyla, Chios.

INTRODUCTORY

St. Nikephoros of Chios was born around 1750 in the town of Kardamyla, in the northeastern part of the famous Aegean island of Chios. He was educated in Chios, taught and wrote in Chios, led a life of spiritual endeavor here, and died here in 1821. He loved Chios as his fatherland, and as a place where piety and learning were flourishing. For this reason, and because no occasion arose for him to leave the island, he remained within its confines throughout his lifetime.

In his childhood, he fell sick of a pestilential disease. His parents, fearing that they might lose him, bound themselves by vow to give him to the celebrated eleventh century Byzantine monastery of Chios known as Nea Moni, if he became well. When he recovered fully, he was taken by them to Nea Moni, and there he became a novice and sub-

sequently a monk. He distinguished himself at
this monastery for his obedience and piety. Having manifested intellectual acuteness and love of
learning, he was sent by the fathers of the monastery to the city of Chios to receive a good education.

Chios was at this time, and up until the year
1822, when the island was devastated by the Turks,
one of the great centers of learning in the Hellenic
world. The School in the city of Chios attracted
students not only from other Aegean islands, but
also from Smyrna, Constantinople, Epiros, Thessaloniki, the Peloponnesos, Crete and even from
non-Greek lands such as Armenia, Syria, Palestine
and Egypt. It had an extremely good library and
excellent teachers, among them Athanasios Parios,
its Director, who taught theology, metaphysics,
rhetoric and logic, and Dorotheos Proios, who
taught mathematics and physics. Before Parios and
Proios, another remarkable educator, Neophytos
Kafsokalyvitis, had taught at this School. Kafsokalyvitis, a Jewish convert to Orthodoxy, had lived
as a monk on Athos, and in 1749 became the first
Director of the school of higher learning that was
established there, named the Athonias Academy.
Subsequently he taught in Chios and then in

Wallachia and Transylvania. He authored many books. According to the historian Constantine Sathas (1842-1914), Neophytos was in Transylvania in 1770.[1] Hence, his stay in Chios must have been sometime after 1749 and before 1770. Sophronios Eustratiadis, author of the important *Hagiology of the Orthodox Church*, says that St. Nikephoros received schooling from Kafsokalyvitis.[2] The historiographer and head of the Gymnasion of Chios George Zolotas (1845-1906), whose five-volume *History of Chios* is one of our main sources of information regarding St. Nikephoros, remarks that it is very probable that Nikephoros received instruction from Neophytos.[3] Zolotas mentions also the following as teachers of the Saint: the priest-teacher Gabriel Astrakaris, the learned preacher Iakovos Mavros, St. Macarios of Corinth, and Athanasios Parios.[4] His education under these teachers was unusually good, and qualified him to become a teacher at the School of Chios. He taught here both before it was reorganized by Parios about 1788 and afterward, for a period of some twenty years.

The influence of St. Macarios of Corinth on St. Nikephoros surpasses by far that of his other teachers. He met St. Macarios before meeting

Parios, as the latter came to Chios eight years after the Corinthian Saint. Macarios first went to Chios in 1780. After some time here, he went to Patmos, thence to Hydra and to Corinth. He returned to Chios and made it his permanent place of residence. From 1790 to 1805, the year of his repose, St. Macarios dwelt at a hermitage named Saint Peter, at Resta. Nikephoros used to see Macarios frequently, in order to receive guidance and inspiration. In 1803, he joined Macarios at Resta, and dwelt here during the rest of his life, following the example of his great mentor. Having the highest esteem for St. Macarios, he sought to have him officially recognized as a Saint by writing his akoluthia. The following hymn from this akoluthia gives eloquent expression to Nikephoros' high regard for him:

> "Rejoice, having through spiritual practices preserved intact the image of the Creator and courageously set, O God-loving one, the intellect, thy ruler, in opposition to pernicious passions, subjugated what is worse to what is better, and made the flesh subject to the Spirit through thine unyielding struggles; and having returned and attained to the state

of likeness-to-God as it was, O Holy
Father, and now enjoying *theosis,* cease
not interceding with God that His great
mercy be granted to our souls."

St. Macarios not only provided the Chian Saint
with a splendid examplar of Orthodox spirituality,
with valuable counsel and instruction in the Orthodox faith, but also with the incitement to write
and to edit works for edifying his Christian breth-
ren. The first work of Nikephoros, an akoluthia
in honor of St. Nicholas the Chian, who suffered
martyrdom in 1754, was in all probability written
at the exhortation of St. Macarios. It appeared in
1799 in the *New Martyrologion* that was compiled
by St. Macarios and edited and completed by St.
Nicodemos the Hagiorite. Also, we know that in
1805, at his deathbed, Macarios entrusted to Nikephoros the completion, editing and publication of
his *New Leimonarion,* "New Spiritual Meadows,"
a monumental book containing the lives and akoluthias of many saints, especially martyrs. In the
New Leimonarion we read that it was at the exhortation of Macarios of Corinth that Nikephoros
corrected in diction and composition the life of St.
Matrona and the akoluthia in honor of St. Gerasimos the New of Kephallenia, both of which are

included in that book. Thus, the development of
St. Nikephoros into a religious writer, and specifi-
cally a writer of sacred poetry and lives of saints,
owes much to the exhortation of St. Macarios.

To Athanasios Parios, who was one of the leading Greek educators of this period, a distinguished
theologian, and a prolific writer who authored
akoluthias, lives of saints and many other types of
works, Nikephoros of Chios also owes much. In-
deed, next to the influence of St. Macarios on his
his development, that of Parios was the greatest.
From Parios he acquired much sacred and secular
knowledge, and it was probably from him that he
learned the art of writing akoluthias. Parios composed the akoluthia of St. Gregory Palamas, that
of the neomartyr Demetrios of Chios, and those of
the martyrs Eleutherios, Phanourios, and Paraskeve. Like Macarios, Parios served for Nikephoros as an exemplar of Christian morality.
Parios, on his part, thought highly of Nikephoros,
both as a person and as an educator; and when he
reorganized the School of Chios, he appointed
Nikephoros a teacher here. In his account of St.
Macarios of Corinth, Parios speaks of Nikephoros
as a most holy priest-monk and a spiritual father
(*pneumatikos pater*) .

Macarios of Corinth and Parios were leading Kollyvades, emphasizing strict adherence to the Orthodox Christian Tradition, to the dogmas, holy canons, and mysteries ('sacraments') of the Orthodox Church, frequent holy communion, and the cultivation of the interior life, especially mental prayer. St. Nikephoros became a devoted follower of them in this regard.[5]

Among others who were close to the Saint over a long period of time was a well-known hermit named Nilos Kalognomos, a Chiot. Nilos, too, was a Kollyvas. Like St. Macarios and Parios, he left Mount Athos when the anti-Kollyvades commotion broke out there. He went to Patmos; and after some time there, to Chios. Together with Nikephoros, he built the Church of St. George at Resta, a solitary region of Chios, and formed here a small monastic community. In his life of St. Macarios of Corinth, Parios speaks of Nilos Kalognomos as "a person having the same convictions and the same sentiments" as St. Macarios; while Zolotas calls Kalognomos "a follower of Macarios."[6] Kalognomos apparently was older than Nikephoros, as Zolotas calls the latter a disciple of Kalognomos.[7]

The influence of the ideas and practices of the Kollyvades on St. Nikephoros is manifested in his writings in such ways as his strong censure of the introduction of the *filioque* into the Creed by the Latin Church, and of the doctrines of the primacy and infallibility of the Pope; and also in his espousal of the hesychast or mystical teaching of the Orthodox Church, evident in his way of life and in his writings. Numerous texts containing these teachings had been collected in the *Philokalia* by his spiritual guide St. Macarios, who published this work, after it had been edited by St. Nicodemos the Hagiorite, in 1782.

As we noted, St. Nikephoros never left Chios. He acquired all his learning in Chios, thanks to the instruction, guidance and inspiration of the teachers that have been mentioned, and also to his extensive reading throughout his life. As far as his reading is concerned, we know that the *New Martyrologion* by Sts. Macarios and Nicodemos was one of his favorite books. He refers to it with admiration in his writings; and as we have seen, he contributed an akoluthia to it. He knew by heart the contents of the *New Leimonarion,* which he completed and edited. In all probability, he read the rest of the writings that St. Macarios of

Corinth compiled, wrote or published, such as the *Philokalia, Concerning Continual Communion* and *Evergetinos,* and also the writings of his other great teacher, Parios, some of which he mentions and praises in one of his published speeches which I shall discuss later. That he read St. Nicodemos' monumental *Synaxaristes,* "Collection of Lives of Saints," is testified by the fact that his name appears in the list of subscribers contained in the third volume of this work.[8] He had great admiration for another of his contemporaries, the outstanding theologian and educator Nikephoros Theotokis, author of remarkable *Kyriakodromia,* "Sunday Sermonaries," that are still widely read in Greece. He refers to him as "the great Theotokis, who is in every respect admirable."[9] In his writings, prose and poetic, St. Nikephoros shows familiarity with the writings of Greek Church Fathers such as St. Basil the Great, St. John Chrysostom, St. Gregory the Theologian and St. Mark of Ephesus, and full acceptance of their authority. Further, he shows great admiration for Homer, Thucydides, Demosthenes and other ancient Greek writers, and evidently had to some extent studied their works.

Sometime after completing his formal education, St. Nikephoros was ordained deacon and later priest at Nea Moni, and also was appointed a teacher in the schools of Chios. During the entire period when he was a teacher, that is, until 1802, he served also as a preacher, teaching the word of God in the city of Chios and at Nea Moni.

It is not known what subjects Nikephoros taught. His biographers are silent on this matter. But we may safely assert that among the subjects he taught was religion, since he was a very pious monk, who in word and deed emphasized that primacy should be given to sacred over secular learning. Of other subjects, he probably taught rhetoric, as he assigns singular importance to it, as we shall see later.

A very informative and eloquent description of the School of Chios and its contributions is contained in two public addresses of St. Nikephoros, one of which was delivered at that school, and the other at the school of the teacher Niketas Kontaratos. Both addresses were delivered in 1802, and first appeared in print in 1926, in George Zolotas' *History of Chios*. They are encomia to 'culture-loving' (*philomousos*) Chios. In both addresses, exhibiting a profound realization, quite reminis-

cent of St. Cosmas Aitolos, of the great importance
of having *schools* in which sacred and secular
studies are combined, Nikephoros rejoices over
the existence and achievements of the School of
Chios, and the appearance of similar schools in
many parts of Greece. "Behold," he says, "schools
are opening everywhere; behold, teachers, who are
founts of every kind of learning, are daily increasing in number in Greece, providing her with their
life-bearing waters."[10] Not only Chios, but also
Smyrna and Kydoniai (Aivali) are doing wonders
in the field of education, he goes on to say, and all
of Greece is filled with enthusiasm.[11] "If you were
to go back not three hundred, or two hundred, or
one hundred, or even fifty years, but only twenty-
five years, you would find only one or two schools,[12]
and in these only instruction in the language being
offered."[13] But now, he says, not only such instruction is offered, but also courses in logic, rhetoric,
metaphysics, theology and also in many sciences.

The School of Chios, he remarks, has secular
wisdom (*epigeios sophia*) *united with* heavenly
wisdom (*ouranios sophia*) or religion (*theosebia*);
but it has heavenly wisdom as its "beginning, root
and foundation, for the fear of the Lord is the beginning of wisdom."[14] This School prepares, he

says, "priests worthy of the altar, preachers capable
of the pulpit, confessors qualified to confess, wise
lawgivers and judges for the order and good ad-
ministration of cities," and also teachers.[15] The
teachers of many Greek schools, he observes, are
graduates of this School.[16]

Like Sts. Cosmas Aitolos, Macarios of Corinth,
and Nicodemos the Hagiorite, St. Nikephoros at-
taches great importance to *books*. In his address
at the School of Chios, he praises it for having
published, within a period of only twenty years,
innumerable books for schools and for the general
public.

In his second address, Nikephoros pays special
tribute to the School for its revival of the art of
rhetoric. Enslavement to the Turks, he remarks,
cast this very valuable art into oblivion; but Chios
has brought it back to the light, through its newly
established School. The methods of rhetoric have
again become known, and its great power has been
revealed.[17] Rhetoric, he says, is the art "by which
and through which were composed the powerful
speeches of Demosthenes, and also those of Aes-
chines, of Lysias, of Livanios, and of all those who
have served as canons and models of eloquence."[18]

It is the art of rhetoric, that "has elevated to, and established in, the intelligible firmament all those luminaries of the world whose special skill was eloquent speech, I mean the Basils, the Gregories, the Chrysostoms."[19]

The man who revived this art in Chios, it should be explained, was Athanasios Parios. The latter wrote a synopsis of Hermogenes' (fl. 2nd century A.D.) book, *The Art of Rhetoric*,[20] revised and completed it at certain points, and also wrote analyses of three orations by Demosthenes. He published this synopsis, together with his analyses of Demosthenes' orations and a study by Livanios, in a volume to which he gave the title *Treatise on Rhetoric*.[21] This book appeared in print in 1799 at Venice. The revival of rhetoric which Parios initiated gained momentum. Thus, in 1807 Korais published the orations of Isocrates in two volumes. In 1813, another Chian, Neophytos Vamvas, published a *Rhetoric*. And the same year, another distinguished educator, the theologian Constantine Oikonomos, published a book entitled *The Art of Rhetoric*.

St. Nikephoros' dwelling on rhetoric, in his discussion of the achievements of the School of Chios,

can be understood properly if we keep in mind
that he was a writer, a teacher and preacher, and
as such was greatly interested in the mastery of the
methods of good expression and successful com-
munication. It might be pointed out in this connection, that the greatest modern Greek missionary, St. Cosmas Aitolos, who was an older con-
temporary of St. Nikephoros, also showed due recognition of the value of rhetoric. In his life by his
disciple Sapphiros Christodoulidis, we read that
before he set out as a missionary he received some
instruction in rhetoric from his brother Chrysan-
thos, who was an educator, "so that he might know
how to speak somewhat methodically."[22]

The two discourses of St. Nikephoros, of which
I have spoken, are also of considerable interest in
relation to two other subjects: *philosophy* and
science. He does not condemn their introduction
into the School. On the contrary, he rejoices over
the fact that so many 'scholastic,' as he calls them,
and so many scientific studies had been added in
recent years to the curriculums of Greek schools,
including that of Chios. Now the term 'scholastic
studies' (*scholastika mathemata*) meant at that
time logic, rhetoric, metaphysics, and theology.[23]
These subjects, as I have already noted, were

taught by Parios. Some of them were probably taught by others, too.

There are no suggestions in the addresses of St. Nikephoros or elsewhere that he taught logic or metaphysics. But it is quite likely, as I remarked earlier, that he taught rhetoric as well as some form of theology. As regards the value of metaphysics, there is also a passage in the second address, in which he asserts that Parios' book devoted to this subject is praiseworthy and much needed.[24] With respect to the sciences, it is worth noting that at the time when St. Nikephoros delivered his two addresses, there were taught in Chios, by the well-trained scientist John Tselepis, the mathematical and physical sciences, including astronomy. Tselepis studied these sciences at the Univerity of Pisa for fifteen years, and taught them at the School of Chios from 1799 to 1821.[25]

One more thing that should be noted in connection with St. Nikephoros' addresses is that there is no trace in them of hostility towards ancient Greek learning — a hostility which some erroneously think is proper to a true Christian. On the contrary, there are expressions, as we have already seen, of great admiration for such repre-

sentatives of it as Homer, Thucydides, and Demosthenes. He speaks of Homer as renowned
for his wisdom;[26] of Thucydides, as a "most truth-
loving, most wise, and excellent writer;" of Demosthenes, as the greatest orator of Greece, and
among those who are canons and models of the
art of rhetoric.[27] With regard to the works of
these and other ancient Greek writers, the Chian
Saint would have given the same advice as has
been given by St. Basil in his *Address to Young
Men*: Select from them whatever is true, incites
to virtue and dissuades from vice; pass over the
rest.

The career of St. Nikephoros as a teacher at the
School of Chios ended in 1802 or early 1803, when
he was elected abbot of Nea Moni. The monastery
was in financial difficulties, owing to poor admin-
istration of its estates; and the Saint, who was
always self-denying and completely trustworthy,
was regarded as the ideal person to rectify its
finances. At Nea Moni, he undertook to educate
the monks, both through formal instruction and
through regular preaching and his example. He
endeavored to train them in justice and in every
other virtue.[28]

Despite his many responsibilities as abbot, he found time to write the history of Nea Moni and a beautiful akoluthia in honor of its founders: the monks Niketas, John, and Joseph. These were published together in 1804 at Venice, in a fine book of 136 pages that has the following rather long title: *The Divine and Holy Akoluthia of Our Holy and God-inspired Fathers Niketas, John and Joseph, Founders of the Venerable, Holy, Royal and Cross-possessing Monastery Named the New, which is Dedicated to Our All-Holy Lady Theotokos and Evervirgin Mary, and the History of the Monastery and Certain Strange Miracles Performed by the Mother of the Lord.* This book is of great historical interest. It has preserved much information about Nea Moni, including many excerpts from imperial chrysobulls, which perished when the Turks devastated Chios in 1822, and a detailed description of the katholikon or main church of the monastery, including its iconographic decoration. Regarding the description of the katholikon, Zolotas observes: "A good description of the church is also provided by the two Giustiniani, and by the travelers Tournefort, Thevenot, and Dallaway; but Nikephoros of Chios surpasses all in simplicity and clear detail. . . . His description has in addition the valuable feature that it was written prior to the destructive events of 1822 and 1881."[29]

This work was translated by abbot Gregory Photinos from the vernacular into older Greek diction, and was published by him in 1865 in Chios as the first part of his *Neamonesia*. Photinos gives additional information about chrysobulls of Nea Moni, having found in the island of Samos, in the Monastery of the Prophet Elias (formerly a dependency of Nea Moni), a number of chrysobulls pertaining to Nea Moni that had not come to the attention of St. Nikephoros. The akoluthia has been reprinted in the fourth edition of the *New Leimonarion* and in the *New Chian Leimonarion*, of which I shall speak later.

The appointment of the Saint as abbot was for two years; but he left before completing this period, and went to the hermitage of St. George at Resta. Zolotas refers to this hermitage as a "small monastery" (*monydrion*).[30] His reason for leaving was, on the one hand, the fact that he found the responsibilities of managing the estates of the monastery exhausting, and on the other, the fact that those under him resisted his efforts to improve their spiritual condition, engaging in cunning and quarrels.

He dwelt at Resta during the rest of his life —
for a period of about eighteen years. His com-
panions here were another retired priest-teacher,
named Joseph, Nilos Kalognomos, and Macarios
of Corinth. A native of Fourna in Agrapha, Thessaly, Joseph led for a time a life of spiritual endeavor on the Holy Mountain of Athos. He appears to have left Athos as a result of the anti-
Kollyvades agitations. After living for a number
of years in Samos, Ikaria and Patmos, he settled in
Chios. A man of learning, Joseph composed an
akoluthia in honor of the hosiomartyr Nicholas the
New, which was published in 1791 at Venice, and
taught for an unknown period of time at the
School of Chios, before he withdrew to the hermitage at Resta.[31] In 1812, Athanasios Parios,
having retired as Director of the schools of Chios,
joined Nikephoros at this small monastery.

The Chian Saint devoted himself here to askesis,
study and writing, strengthened by the compan-
ionship and counsel of the holy men I have just
mentioned. He engaged in all those activities that
distinguish the life of a pious Orthodox monk,
such as regular daily worship at church, private
prayer, reading sacred books, vigils, strict fasts,
tiring prostrations, and manual work. Having as

his supreme aim *theosis* — union with God, participation in His perfection and blessedness — he used
the most effective means to this end: inner attention and unceasing mental prayer, as one can
gather from reading his works.

His withdrawal to the wilderness did not result
in his forgetting the people who lived in the city
and the villages of Chios. He prayed for them,
visited them from time to time to preach to them,
to confess them, or to help them in their sickness.
And they did not forget him. Many came to his
hermitage to confess, to receive counsel, or to ask
for material aid.

With regard to his manual work, it should be
noted that one important form of it was agriculture. St. Nikephoros planted innumerable olive
and fig-trees, pines and cypresses, and developed
a nursery. A great lover of trees, and deeply conscious of their value in the material welfare of
man, he urged all to plant trees. Like St. Cosmas
Aitolos, he had a keen realization that lack of trees
was a source of extreme poverty and wretchedness,
and that planting of trees was an important means
of increasing one's material resources. In one of
his prophecies, St. Cosmas says: "Men will become

poor because they will not have love for trees."[32]
St. Nikephoros saw this happen in Chios; and he
used every opportunity, including his sermons and
confession, to urge the Chiots to plant trees. Often,
for penance he would tell his confessant to plant
so many trees. In order to encourage and help
people to plant trees, he used to give away to all
trees from his nursery at Resta. To induce some
men to plant trees, he would go so far as to reward
them with money — money he had gained by sell-
ing the property he had inherited from his father.

At the hermitage, the Saint also occupied himself with writing, as I have already noted. It was
here that he fulfilled the task which St. Macarios
had entrusted him with at his deathbed, in April
of 1805: the editing and completion of his *New
Leimonarion,* a book containing the lives and akoluthias of martyrs and other saints, men and
women. Nikephoros worked on this over a period
of many years. He arranged the material in the
best order, improved the diction and composition,
made various corrections, wrote additional lives
and akoluthias, oikoi to St. Matrona of Chios, and
a number of troparia which he inserted in akoluthias that had been authored by others. A prod-
uct of the collaboration of two saints and a dis-

tinguished theologian and scholar, Parios, who contributed the Preface, a number of lives, akoluthias and other material, this book is one of the most remarkable religious works that has come out of Chios. It first appeared in print in 1819, two years before the repose of St. Nikephoros, and has been reprinted thrice — between 1855 and 1857 at Hermoupolis (in the island of Syros), in three volumes, and in 1873 and 1913 at Athens. The title *New Leimonarion* is followed in the first edition by this subtitle: *Containing old and new martyrdoms and lives of holy ascetics which were collected by the blessed Metropolitan of Corinth Saint Macarios Notaras, to which have been added the lives of saints contained in the Triodion and in the Pentekostarion, translated by the most learned teacher, master Athanasios Parios, and further, akoluthias designed to be chanted in honor of various neomartyrs, composed by the Very Reverend Nikephoros of Chios for the benefit of all the Orthodox.* It is a folio book in two parts, the first part made up of 328 pages and the second of 152 pages. Part Two contains the akoluthias and lives of saints who are more particularly celebrated in Chios.

A substantial part of the *New Leimonarion* has

appeared in the *New Chian Leimonarion,* which was published at Athens in 1930 and again in 1968. The latter contains some new material, in particular, the life and akoluthia of St. Nikephoros of Chios. The second edition contains also the life and akoluthia of St. Nectarios, the famous twentieth century saint who was tonsured a monk at Nea Moni and served as a school-teacher in one of the villages of Chios for seven years. Left out of the *New Chian Leimonarion* are the Preface (*Proanaphonesis*) by Athanasios Parios, and the lives and akoluthias of a number of saints who are unrelated to Chios. Some of the latter were written by St. Nikephoros.

Included in the original *New Leimonarion* are the following writings by our Saint: nine lives, a dozen akoluthias, and a number of other hymnographical works. The lives are those of the martyr Myrope and of the neomartyrs Demetrios the Peloponnesian, Luke the New, Theophilos, John of Thessaloniki, Lazarus the Bulgar, Angelis, George of Chios, and Markella of Chios. The akoluthias are of these saints, with the exception of John of Thessaloniki, and those of the holy ascetics Gerasimos the New and Matrona, and of the neomartyrs Mark the New and George of Ephesus.

The fact that Nikephoros used his literary talents and skill for writing lives of saints and akoluthias in honor of them shows that he assigned great value to such works. He evidently felt very strongly that such writings provide splendid examplars, inciting many to emulation. In the Induction to the akoluthia in honor of the founders of Nea Moni — Niketas, John, and Joseph — he observes that the lives of these saints "had never been placed on the lampstand of the printed work, in order to shine upon the whole of Christendom." Emily Sarou, his biographer, remarks that these words make it clear how much he desired to see the lives and deeds of those who practiced true and integral Christian virtue collected and presented to all; and she adds that he contributed a great deal towards this end.[33]

He admired most two categories of saints: ascetics, or spiritual strivers who withdrew to the wilderness and led a life of inner stillness (*hesychia*) and prayer, and martyrs. Four of the saints about whom he wrote were ascetics: Macarios of Corinth, and Niketas, John and Joseph, founders of Nea Moni; the rest were martyrs.

St. Nikephoros' lives of saints and his akoluthias

and other sacred poetry are sublime works, full of lofty thoughts and pervaded by elevated feelings. They convey a vivid picture of the life and character of the saints they are devoted to. Also, they give eloquent expression to the Orthodox view of God and of man; to the splendor of the virtues of faith, hope, love, wisdom, humility, chastity, courage, and so on. Further, they are permeated with the ideas of the *Philokalia,* such as *theosis,* effulgence, illumination, contemplation, catharsis, passionlessness, inner wakefulness, unceasing mental prayer or prayer of the heart, and holy askesis in general.

With regard to God, I note that St. Nikephoros speaks of Him as the Creator *(Poietes, Ktistes)* of all things, visible and invisible, ruler of all, almighty, immaterial, unchanging, a consubstantial Trinity: Father, Son, and Holy Spirit. God is for him transcendentally good, all-merciful, a lover of man *(philanthropos)*. The Saint describes Christ as the beginningless Logos of God, consubstantial with the Father, begotten of the Father before all ages. Christ ineffably became incarnate, assuming the nature of man, and is the renewer and Savior of man. Nikephoros speaks often of the Holy Spirit as the giver of grace, strengthening man spiritu-

ally, sanctifying the soul and the body, bestowing
the gifts of prophecy and of performing miracles.
Thoroughly Orthodox in his theology, he em-
phatically rejects the view that the Holy Spirit
proceeds from the *Son* as well as from the Father.[34]

Of the attributes of God, the Saint mentions
most often His creativity, His mercifulness, and
His love of man.

The prose and poetic works of St. Nikephoros
convey not only a theology, but also an anthro-
pology, a teaching regarding man's nature and
destiny. Man is a dual being, composed of soul
and body. However, he is chiefly a soul. Hence,
innumerable hymns end as prayers for the "salvation of our souls."

Man's soul has distinct faculties or powers. The
'rational faculty' (*nous, dianoia*) and the 'heart'
(*kardia*) are the ones which the Saint mentions
most often. He dwells on the rational faculty in
its *intuitive* aspect. Contemplation (*theoria*) is
by *nous* or *dianoia*: these two terms are used inter-
changeably. Effulgence (*ellampsis*), illumination
(*photismos*) pertains to this faculty, which is the
master power (*hegemon*). The heart is the seat

of faith, of the feelings, lower as well as higher, such as spiritual love and joy. Another important power is 'conscience' (*syneidesis*). Conscience censures us when we do what is morally wrong, and prompts us to repent.

In addition to these powers, there are in the soul certain 'passions' (*pathe*). There are passions that are purely psychical, such as pride, and there are others which are psychophysical, such as lust. Both kinds of passions cloud the rational faculty and defile the heart. The saints are described as having opposed them, cleansed themselves of them, and attained complete freedom from passions (*apatheia*).

St. Nikephoros speaks also of 'thoughts' (*logismoi*). Some of these are good, others are evil, soul-corrupting; some are from God, others are from demons. The saints are exhibited by him as having cleansed themselves from all evil thoughts, and as having heeded and cultivated the good.

Catharsis, 'purification' from the passions and bad thoughts, is viewed by him as a necessary condition for growth in the virtues. Through the development of the virtues, man attains likeness to God. And through likeness, *theosis,* 'deification,' is attained. *Theosis* is union with God, participation in God's perfection, glory and blessedness through grace. This state is presented by Nikephoros as man's highest goal, one which the saints attained in this life, and in which they abide now and will abide forever.

A few words should be said about the *form* of St. Nikephoros' poetry. He follows faithfully the traditional Greek Orthodox models in his akoluthias and other poetic works. Each akoluthia is divided into two parts: the part which consists of hymns that are chanted during the great vespers (*megas hesperinos*), and the part which consists of hymns that are chanted during the matins (*orthros*). The second part is longer than the first. Both parts are made up of a considerable number of hymns, composed in such a way as to be chanted in a particular mode of Byzantine chant, such as the First Mode, the Second Mode, etc.,[35] or as to be chanted *like* some other well-known hymn, and called *prosomoia*. Some of the hymns are addressed to the Holy Trinity; others, to Christ; others, to the Theotokos; and others, the majority, to the particular saint whose memory is celebrated. The hymns which St. Nikephoros composed for his akoluthias, and those which he composed and inserted in akoluthias written by others, show excellence of diction and very careful observance of form, rendering them easy to execute and delightful to hear. Also, they are rich and sublime in content.

The twenty-four *Oikoi* to St. Matrona of Chios constitute a church service in honor of this Saint. They are modeled after the Salutations to the Theotokos contained in the Akathistos Hymn. An *oikos* in Byzantine hymnography is a strophe that follows a *kontakion* — a short hymn which summarizes the significance of the holy day or saint that is celebrated. The kontakion in this service is preceded by a troparion and followed by twenty-four oikoi, each of which is accompanied by a group of twelve verses that begin with the word *Chaire*, "Rejoice," and the refrain: "Rejoice O glorious Matrona." The service closes with a repetition of the kontakion. The troparion, the kontakion, the refrains and the alleluias are chanted by the choir, while the oikoi and the accompanying verses are recited by the priest in an intoned voice. The service is as carefully and elegantly composed and as rich and uplifting in content as the other poetic compositions of the Chian Saint.

His productivity as a composer of liturgical poetry, the superior quality of his compositions, as regards both form and content, place St. Nikephoros among the major hymnographers of the Greek Church of the last two hundred years.

Like Macarios of Corinth, Nikephoros is of considerable importance as a 'trainer of martyrs' (*aleiptes martyron*).[36] Many who had abjured their Christian faith and embraced Islam, and then repented for this act, went to St. Nikephoros at the recommendation of pious Orthodox Christians who held him in the highest esteem for his holiness. They went to him to confess their sin and to be prepared by him to endure martyrdom, in order to wipe away the sin of apostasy. For reflecting on the statement of Christ that "Whoever shall deny me before men, him will I also deny before my Father Who is in Heaven,"[37] they felt that only by boldly affirming their faith in Christ before the Moslem authorities could they be fully cleansed of their sin. St. Nikephoros' part as a 'trainer of martyrs' was not only to confess them, but also to enlighten them as much as possible in matters of the faith, to prescribe for them an austere form of discipline (e.g. fasts, prostrations, unceasing prayer), and to instill in them unyielding fortitude. Thus prepared, they endured with amazing courage the cruel tortures to which they were subjected by the Turks, and finally submitted to death, for the sake of their Orthodox Christian faith and the salvation of their souls. Among these were St. Theodore of Byzantium and St. Demetrios the Peloponnesian,[38] who were also trained by Macarios of Corinth. The neomartyr Theodore suffered martyrdom in 1795, in Mytilene; Demetrios, in 1803, in Tripolis of the Peloponnesos. Another was St. Mark the New, who suffered martyrdom in 1801, in Chios.[39] Still another was St. Angelis of Argos, who was martyred in Chios in 1813.[40] Nikephoros personally prepared for martyrdom others, too, whose names have not been preserved.[41] And he incited and prepared many others for martyrdom through his published lives and akoluthias of martyrs.

His efforts in this regard sprang from his deep conviction in the great value of enduring martyrdom for the sake of the true faith, both for the martyr himself and for the faithful who take cognizance of it. Through martyrdom, the martyr becomes a recipient of Divine grace, is purified of all taint of sin and is sanctified, receiving heavenly glory and honor. Also, through martyrdom, faith

is revitalized in people, and they become "martyrs in choice," as St. Basil the Great says, by ad-
miring the martyrs and honoring them by means
of hymns.[42]

Like Sts. Cosmas Aitolos and Macarios of Corinth, St. Nikephoros had the gift of working miracles. He is credited with the performance of
miracles both during his lifetime and after his
repose. In his biography by Emily Sarou, we read
that he was often asked by the peasants of Chios
in times of drought to pray for rain and that almost always it rained soon after, occasioning great
joy in the people. Also, we read in it that he cured
many persons promptly by placing on them a relic
of St. Macarios, which he carried with him; and
further, that he cured many others of himself,
among them two who suffered from insanity.

The gift of working miracles was undoubtedly
one of the factors that resulted in the early recognition of Nikephoros as a Saint. But no less important factors were his holy way of life, which
has already been described, and his saintly character. According to the Orthodox view, a saint is
a person who is free of every vice and the possessor
of all the virtues, having become a partaker of

Divine grace. St. Nikephoros was adorned with every moral and spiritual virtue. But the excellences that the people of Chios especially took notice of were his humility, his gentleness, his total freedom from anger, his love for his fellow men, particularly as manifested in forgiveness, in compassion, in almsgiving.[43]

Nikephoros was regarded as a Saint by the Chiots even in his lifetime. He began to be celebrated as a saint in Chios in 1845, when his relics were removed from the grave, following a dream which the monk Agathangelos of Hydra saw. In 1845, this monk, who dwelt at Resta, saw in a dream the place where the Saint had been buried. He dug there and found the relics. Upon hearing this, a sick man named Nicholas Lodis, who resided in the village of Vrontados, began invoking the Saint to help him recover his health, and one day he saw St. Nikephoros in a dream. He was instructed by the Saint to go to his opened grave and take some soil. Accordingly, this man, who was suffering dreadfully, was carried there. He took some soil and promptly became well. Full of gratitude and exultation, he commissioned a painter to make an icon of the Saint in accordance with the description which he gave, based on the appearance of the Saint in the dream.[44] This, so far as is known, was the first icon of St. Nikephoros.

The day chosen by the Chiots in 1845 for commemorating St. Nikephoros was May 1st. They continued to commemorate him regularly on that day unofficially until 1907. That year they began to celebrate his memory on May 1st *officially*. A beautiful large icon of the Saint was made in 1907, in the likeness of the icon that was done in 1845, and was placed in the Church of St. George at Resta. Also, his akoluthia and life were written and published in 1907. The akoluthia was composed by Kyrillos Trehakis, Protosyngellos[45] of the Metropolitan of Chios, while the biography was written by Emily Sarou, daughter of George Zolotas, who wrote the five-volume *History of Chios*.

Both the akoluthia and the biography bear vivid testimony to the sainthood of Nikephoros. In the hymns of the akoluthia, Trehakis says that Nikephoros attained perfection. Having "from childhood diligently practiced virtue," he became "a most precise rule of virtue," a "divine model of monastics," "an instrument of the Holy Spirit," "a great teacher of the faithful," "a pillar of the Church."[46]

Although far from having received the recognition which they deserve, the holy life and sacred writings of St. Nikephoros have been receiving increasing attention with the passage of time. Since 1907, his life by Sarou has been reprinted twice: in the *New Chian Leimonarion* of 1930 and in that of 1968. A somewhat abridged and revised version of this life, together with the Saint's apolytikion, kontakion and three megalynaria by Trehakis have appeared in the fifth volume of Victor Matthaiou's *Great Synaxaristes,* "Great Collection of Lives of Saints," in the 1962 and the later editions. Also, a biographical sketch of the Saint is contained in Eustratiadis' *Hagiology of the Orthodox Church,* which was published in 1960, and in the more recent Greek *Religious and Ethical Encyclopedia.*[47]

Further, some of the lives of martyrs which he wrote have been incorporated in the *Great Synaxaristes* of Constantine Doukakis and in that of Victor Matthaiou.

Though the poetic creations of St. Nikephoros

have not received the attention they merit, they certainly have not remained altogether unnoticed by Greek and Western scholars. Thus, in his *Hagiology of the Orthodox Church*, Eustratiadis makes reference to nine of the akoluthias composed by the Saint,[48] while Louis Petit lists all of them in his well-documented book, *Bibliographie des acolouthies grecques*, which was published in 1926 at Brussels.

The Orthodox are bound to become increasingly cognizant of the very holy, beautiful, and creative life of St. Nikephoros the Chian and of his extremely edifying writings. More and more will read his biography and his works, and celebrate his memory on May 1st, chanting sublime, joyful hymns, such as the following apolytikion by Kyrillos Trehakis:

> "Thou hast been shown to be, O Nikephoros, a most luminous star of the Church of Christ, an exceedingly rich meadow of His truth, and a mellifluent clarion, delighting the hearts of the faithful with divinely inspired teachings. Wherefore intercede with Christ God for the salvation of our souls."

THE LIFE OF ST. NIKEPHOROS

By Emily Sarou[1]

The name of Saint Nikephoros is known in every corner of Chios, and even outside of Chios among all those Chians who have heard from their fathers and grandfathers about the life of this holy and most virtuous man. He is known to all and is admired by all. But his life has not yet become known to many from beginning to end. Saint Nikephoros has not yet entered the choir of historical persons. The facts about him have never been placed upon the lampstand of the press, thus to shine upon the whole Christian world. They have remained covered up; and with the passage of time their fame and glory have been obscured, and finally have been in danger of being extinguished. We consider it a major duty to his inindefatigable and virtue-loving soul, and also to

47

the modern history of our fatherland, to preserve sacred remembrance of him vivid amongst all of us and amongst those who will come after us.

Our chief source of information about Saint Nikephoros are the notes of the distinguished master of the high school (*gymnasion*) of Chios George Zolotas, who, having great admiration and love for this Saint of Chios, diligently gathered together all the authentic information about the Saint that he could. For he had decided to write the life of the Saint, especially after spending the summer of 1905 in the forest of Resta, which is full of recollections about Nikephoros, and where he died the following year. Having at our disposal these notes and much oral information taken selectively from trustworthy persons, we will sketch faithfully the holy life of Nikephoros.

He was born about 1750, in Kardamyla of Chios. His family name was Georgios.[2] Having fallen sick at an early age of a 'pestilential' disease and been saved, he was 'given as an offering' by his parents to the All-Holy Virgin (*Panagia*) of Nea Moni, that he might serve her. When he recovered fully, he was taken by them to the Monastery and placed under the direction of Anthimos Agiopateritis, "a venerable and wonderful elder," as Saint Nikephoros himself remarks. Later, he was sent to the city of Chios, in order that he might be educated in the schools there by the priest-teacher Gabriel Astrakaris, parish priest of the Church of Saint Eustratios at Vounakion that belonged to Nea Moni. He remained close to this priest-teacher during the entire period of his education in the city, was educated in soul and intellect, and developed love and respect for learning and for those who transmit it — the first indication of a good child, auguring a superior citizen. Throughout all the subsequent stages of his life, there is manifest his reverence towards teachers and love of learning. His love of learning later brought him to Athanasios Parios, while his love of the Christian faith led him to Saint Macarios — the two powerful pillars of education and religion in Chios.

Having completed his education, he returned to the Monastery and was ordained a deacon. Afterward, he was appointed teacher in the schools[3] of Chios, and served in these for many years. At the same time he was a preacher, and went often to Nea Moni also, in order to preach the word of God.

While a teacher, he was called to become abbot

of the Monastery. Here, until 1802, the monks
managed its affairs without any audits. That year,
the Monastery was subjected to the penalty of
600,000 piasters (*grosia*) and, owing to the lack
of money, many landed estates of Nea Moni were
sold. The citizens, suspecting that the manage-
ment of the affairs of the Monastery was not exe-
cuted faithfully, and wishing to bring about an
improvement in its finances, had the holy teacher
Nikephoros made abbot of the Monastery. For he
was devoid of possessions, ascetic and absolutely
trustworthy. Also, they instituted an annual audit
of the accounts of the Monastery, to be made by
the elders of the city in the fall. From this we
learn that Nikephoros went to Nea Moni as abbot
in 1802 or a little after this, and hence that he was
until that year a teacher in the city of Chios.

The abbacy was at that time, owing to the
manifold matters it involved, not something easy,
especially for a man who was not familiar with
such matters, but was a great lover of solitude and
study. Nonetheless, the Saint zealously endeavored to serve the interests of the Monastery, to
bring about a reconciliation where there were
conflicts, and in general to smooth the situation

through his modest good judgment and discernment.

He offered another, no less necessary service in the Monastery: the elevation of the moral spirit of the monks, he himself providing an admirable example. He undertook the regular teaching of the monks, a teaching not of letters, but of deeds and of virtue, especially justice, which he had innate and through education had brought to the perfection in which Aristeides possessed it, as his whole life testifies.

But he evidently grew tired from toiling and persevering in things alien to him, and above all from the ingratitude of those about him and under him. He left and went to Resta, before completing the two-year period as abbot for which he had been elected. For our holy Nikephoros was altogether a stranger to cunning and quarrels, a true philosopher in Christ. Unable to govern in the midst of a tempest of passions, he left for the good haven of virtue.

Now we ask: What constituted a stage of discernment for Nikephoros, to remain abbot, or to withdraw from abbacy, in view of the fact that he was a zealous admirer of contemplatives, and that having failed in governing monks, he did not fail in excelling in his own life and in guiding numerous souls to virtue, even after his death? If we go back in history, we shall find many such examples in similar circumstances. The great Chrysostom must have had in mind a man with a character like that of the holy Nikephoros, when he thundered these immortal words: "How philosophical it is to scorn present things, to regard virtue as something great, not to seek prizes in this life, but to place one's hopes in what lies beyond it, and to have the soul in such an ardent and dedicated state, as not to let present sufferings obstruct our hopes that pertain to the life to come."

Following these divine words, and having as his exemplars the great clerics and men of learning who flourished in Chios earlier and in his own time, and relying also on his own strength of soul, good Nikephoros toiled indefatigably with all his resources, opened a path for himself, and trod it steadfastly towards immortality.

The first example of his devout diligence is the composition and publication of the *Akoluthia of the Holy Fathers Niketas, John and Joseph,* to which is appended the history of Nea Moni and a fine description of its church. This book was published in 1804. At the end of the simple and beautiful Preface, he says: "This small and imperfect work of mine has been read, among others, by the very learned priest-teacher Iakovos Mavros and by my very critical and very venerable teacher Athanasios Parios, and they agreed that it was worthy of being published." And he adds: "If the history of the Monastery has not been clarified sufficiently, please forgive me, realizing that to the extent that it was possible for me to investigate and ascertain things I did not by any means neglect to do so." What modesty of a wealthy host with regard to his rich literary banquet, begging to be forgiven for any imperfections!

How useful his diligence has been in this connection is manifest. For had there not been this inestimable Nikephoros to gather together the data pertaining to Nea Moni and to record its treasures, among which there shone as precious stones the chrysobulls of the Byzantine Emperors who endowed it most abundantly, all of us would have been ignorant of what we know about it at present, inasmuch as shortly after his death all these invaluable pieces of testimony perished.[4] In a word, this book alone would have sufficed to render his name immortal.

His akoluthia in honor of the holy Fathers Niketas, John and Joseph, too, is beautiful. So also
are various other akoluthias and church hymns
which he composed for various occasions, including the salutations (*chairetismoi*) to Saint Matrona of Chios. All of them are full of religious
exaltation and possess high literary merit, for his
strong and lively spirit was richly endowed with
poetic gifts.

Having left Nea Moni, the holy Nikephoros
went to Resta, to his friend Joseph, a priest-
teacher,[5] because Saint Macarios lived in this vi-
cinity. From certain lives of martyrs in the *New
Leimonarion,* it is apparent that Saint Nikephoros
had prior to this been in very frequent touch with
Saint Macarios. Nikephoros and Joseph, together
with the Chian Nilos Kalognomos (who had lived
as a monk on the Holy Mountain of Athos, was a
Kollyvas and a very dear companion of Saint Macarios) dwelt here under the spiritual care and holy
influence of the blessed Macarios during the last
years of his life. Close to Saint Macarios and the
others we have mentioned, there stayed and were
instructed in adherence to the Christian faith some
of the neomartyrs who are included in the *New
Leimonarion.* One of these was Saint Demetrios

the Peloponnesian, whom Saint Nikephoros confessed here, and who suffered martyrdom in 1803 at Tripolis of Arcadia. Saint Mark the New also stayed with them for a number of days, until he was able to find a ship for Kousantasi.[6] Before he was martyred, Saint Angelis often went to Nikephoros and the others who dwelt at Resta, and to the grave of Saint Macarios. Near the divine Nikephoros, who henceforth lived at Resta, there dwelt also, during the remaining brief period of his life, Nikephoros' beloved teacher Athanasios Parios, who in 1812 retired as director of the schools of Chios owing to his old age.[7]

We must imagine the long residence of Saint Nikephoros in its proper setting. With full consciousness of his spiritual and moral powers, he came to this then small forest, which was free of all worldly bustle, having by him both the sublime faith of Saint Macarios and the noble Christian learning of Athanasios Parios. For Athanasios was a model of piety and Christian morality — he was censured by some for not following the supposed progressive spirit of his time.[8] When he was past his fruitful period as an educator, he came here to end his days in tranquillity, in the company of Nikephoros and Joseph,[9] men of virtue and lovers of learning.

In 1819, Saint Nikephoros published in Venice
the *New Leimonarion,* a very remarkable book
that is worthy of careful study. The first collector
of the material contained in this book was Saint
Macarios, who also wrote many of the lives of
saints which it comprises. Athanasios Parios was
a collaborator. He contributed a varied collection
of lives of saints, translated into the vernacular.
Saint Nikephoros, too, wrote many lives of saints
and accompanying akoluthias. Further, he arranged and embellished the whole collection.
When Saint Macarios was dying, the book was in
an unfinished state, and he requested the holy
Nikephoros to complete and edit it. This is evident from the epigram by Saint Nikephoros that
appears at the beginning of the book.

Going over this extremely valuable work of
Saint Nikephoros, we note with how much intelli-
gence, diligence and precision he has compiled
and presented the material. The parts which he
wrote are avowedly the most beautiful, having
been composed with extreme clarity, elegance and
manifest fervor. Throughout them there is evident his boundless love for our Church and our
People, for whose sake he prepared these writings.
He wrote by preference the lives which are con-

nected with Chios: those of Saints Theophilos,[10] Angelis, Markella, and Matrona. But he also wrote others, not related to Chios. In his life of Saint Demetrios the Peloponnesian, he says: "O eros! O longing (for our holy faith)! O ardent love, which no one can experience, but he alone who has cleansed his heart and made it worthy of such love!" He must have felt this utterance very deeply, to have expressed it so vividly. Elsewhere again, in the life of Saint John of Thessaloniki, which is the most beautiful of all, he says: "But he remained undefiled, just as the sun is not defiled when its rays pass through muddy and dirty places." Such resplendent luminaries does the holy Nikephoros place in the difficult and hard-to-imitate lives of the Martyrs; luminaries which, while evincing the sublime spiritual development of the author, simultaneously attract those who hesitate at the beginning of the difficult path, urge them onward, and guide them as they advance.

The Saint dwelt at Resta for about twenty years. He greatly improved the landed estate here, occupying himself in it during this entire period. Thus, he planted pines on the small hills on the right and on the left side, which are such a delightful sight today. The other trees there: olives and

fig-trees (the latter formerly abounded) , as well as
the cypresses, are creations of industrious and tree-
loving Nikephoros. He also developed a nursery
in this estate, and gave away young trees abundantly to all. Going about often in villages, he
incited continually the peasants to plant trees,
giving his blessings and offering his holy prayers
to those who planted young trees. It is known
that he sold the landed estates which he inherited
from his father and used the money he received
from their sale for rewards to those who planted
many olive-trees, both in his native town of Kardamyla and in many other places.

The peasants, particularly those of Kardamyla,
who even today greatly honor his memory, had
such reverence for him and such faith in him that
at times of drought they entreated him to intercede with God. The good intercession was almost
always readily accepted, and the people rejoiced,
seeing on the one hand that venerable elder not
getting tired of doing benevolent acts for them,
and on the other hand wealth-bringing rain com-
ing in response to his prayers. . . .

He went often, as we said, to the city and to
villages, sometimes visiting sick persons, at other

times preaching the word of God with clarity and simplicity, for the real benefit of the people. On such occasions, he urged the people to plant trees. Even in his old age he did not hesitate, but hastened to those who had need of his presence. It is said in the life of Saint Macarios that the holy Nikephoros was sought by a sick woman from Kallimasia, but was not found at the house in the city of Chios where he usually passed the night,[11] having gone to the village of Nenita. So they hastened thither and found him on the way back to the city. They told him the reason why they wanted him, and he went to the sick woman, even though it was nine o'clock in the night and he was very tired. He cured the sick woman instantly, by placing upon her a relic of Saint Macarios which he always carried on himself, and by means of which he often performed miracles to many. But he also performed many miracles of himself. Unfortunately, however, accounts of few of them have come down to us. One of them was performed to a girl who resided at Kallimasia and was mentally deranged. Another was to a madman in Vrontados. He cured both permanently. Another man, Nicholas Lodis of Vrontados, who suffered dreadfully, often invoked the Saint after his repose. One night he saw the Saint in a dream instructing

him to go to his grave and take some soil. This
happened at the time of the removal of the relics
of the Saint from the grave.[12] The next day the
sick man was carried to the grave and took some
soil. Then he had a water-sanctification ceremony
(*hagiasmos*) performed, and thereupon was cured.
Full of gratitude and fervor, he asked a painter to
do the icon of the Saint, depicting him as he had
seen him in the dream. This icon is the one which
was used recently as the model for the large icon
that was made for the church of St. George at
Resta.[13]

At another time, while the Saint was away on a
tour, his goat, the only one he had, was stolen.
When he returned, he found his disciple (*hypo-
taktikos*) sorrowful and angry over the theft. Saint
Nikephoros at once calmed him, saying: "Be not
angry, because the thief must have been poor. We
had the goat long enough; let someone else have
her now." As soon as he had finished saying these
words, the thief arrived weeping. He confessed his
wrong act, and added that he had slaughtered the
goat, but found it impossible to sell the meat.
Saint Nikephoros promptly forgave him, saying:
"Now go back and you will sell the meat." When
this man arrived at his home, he learned from his

wife that during his absence all the meat had been sold.

It is also known that Saint Nikephoros foresaw and foretold all the sufferings that would soon take place.[14]

His goodness and compassion were marvelous. Thus, all the money he received from time to time he gave away to assist the needy, he himself remaining poor. He never gave alms himself, but always through a trustworthy child, whom he instructed to leave the assistance to the suffering family and depart at once. The rest of his way of life, too, was in accordance with the teaching and example of the Gospels.

The hermitage at Resta, whose church he repaired and whose cells he extended, became a center for pilgrims, one from which there radiated the holiness and compassion of the venerable priest. People came to him chiefly to confess, but also to be consoled — each according to his particular unhappy state of soul — and to hear the holy words of God.

He had disciples, '*hypotaktikoi*,' at Resta, of whom we know the names of only three. One of

them was Macarios Garis of Vrontados. After
having been educated and trained by Saint Nikephoros, this disciple was taken in 1817 by Platon,
Metropolitan of Chios, as his archdeacon. He accompanied Platon until the end.[15] Another was
Kyrillos Vavylos, who later became a preacher in
the city of Chios. The third was Michael Lagoutis,
also of Vrontados, who became known as a teacher
of church music.[16]

Saint Nikephoros was, as we know from tradition, of medium stature and well-formed body.
He had a comely pale face, gentle expression,
beautiful eyes and a large black beard.

In all probability he died in the summer of
1821, at the city of Chios, in a home near the
Church of St. Paraskeve, where he used to pass the
night whenever he could not return to Resta on
the same day. His body was brought to Resta and
was placed in the tomb where that of Athanasios
Parios had been buried, and before it that of the
Hagiorite Nilos Kalognomos, which had been
buried there by Saint Nikephoros.

The monk Agathangelos of Hydra, who dwelt
at Resta, saw in a dream in 1845 the place of his
burial. He dug there and found the sacred relics

of the Saint. These were brought to the Metropolitan Church by His Holiness Sophronios, then Metropolitan of Chios and later Patriarch of Alexandria. Here they were kept in a closed case. After many years, the Guild of Tanners, to whom belongs the estate and the church at Resta, asked for the sacred relics and placed them in a beautiful case, which they deposited in the sanctuary (*hieron*) of St. George. They are devoutly venerated by those who come here.

In 1907, the Guild of Tanners, who hold the memory of the Saint in great reverence and honor, placed in this church a beautiful icon of him; and the Very Reverend and learned Kyrillos Trehakis, Chief Assistant (*Protosyngellos*) of the Metropolitan of Chios, composed a beautiful and holy akoluthia in honor of him. At this time, it was decided that May 1st should be the day when Saint Nikephoros should be commemorated.

Such was the life of the holy Nikephoros. Such is the example that he left for us. First he learned and then he eagerly taught others. He preached with fervor everywhere in the island of Chios the words of Jesus Christ. He offered his services at Nea Moni as an impartial brother. Also, he gathered together the data pertaining to the history of Nea Moni, both as an expression of gratitude to it, because "it had taught him letters," and also as an offering to the Greek people, who received this book as an incorruptible torch of the spiritual life. Later, he withdrew to a place of stillness (*hesychia*). Here he occupied himself with the inner development of those about him and of those who came to him, aiding morally and materially those in need. He passed his life in prayer and study, promoting every activity that was conductive to the public good and helping every suffering person. He made such broad and beneficial use of his mission in the world, that he became greatly revered and blessed among men, a pillar of the Church and of the Greek Nation. Not for a moment did he seek for himself worldly glory, as we have seen, and he fled the pleasures of the world and vain preoccupations. He anchored himself far from the turmoil of the world, in a safe harbor, in religion and learning. Here, drawing indomitable powers, he returned to the society of men, whenever they and their needs called him. He instilled into the pains of their souls and bodies the balm which gushed forth from his great Christian heart and the power of his most holy life.

WORKS OF THE SAINT

BOOKS

(1) *He Theia kai Hiera Akolouthia ton Hosion kai Theophoron Pateron hemon Niketa, Ioannou kai Ioseph, ton Ktitoron tes en Chio Sebasmias, Hieras, Basilikes te kai Stauropegiakes Mones tes Epilegomenes Neas, tes ep' Onomati Timomenes tes Hyperagias Despoines hemon Theotokou kai Aeiparthenou Marias, e te Historia tes Mones kai Thaumata Tina Paradoxa para tes Theometoros Telesthenta* ("The Divine and Holy Akoluthia of Our Holy and God-inspired Fathers Niketas, John and Joseph, Founders of the Venerable, Holy, Royal and Cross-possessing Monastery Named the New, Which is Dedicated to Our All-Holy Lady

65

Theotokos and Evervirgin Mary, and the History of the Monastery and Certain Strange Miracles Performed by the Mother of the Lord"). Venice, 1804. 2nd ed. in *Ta Neamonesia* ("Writings Pertaining to Nea Moni"), by Gregorios Photeinos, Book I, Chios, 1865.

(2) *Neon Leimonarion* ("New Spiritual Meadows"). Edited and completed by the Saint. Venice, 1819. 2nd ed., in 3 vols., Hermoupolis, Syros, 1855-1857; 3rd ed. Athens, 1873; 4th ed., Athens, 1913. Revised ed. (considerable material has been omitted, and some new material has been added), with the title *Neon Chiakon Leimonarion* ("New Chian Leimonarion"), edited by Amvrosios Michalos, Athens, 1930, and by Christophoros K. Gerazounis, Athens, 1968.

DISCOURSES

(1) *Logos Enkomiastikos eis ten Theotokon* ("Discourse of Praise to the Theotokos"). Published in the *New Leimonarion* and the *New Chian Leimonarion*.

(2) *Logos Enkomiastikos e Enkomion pros ten Philomouson Chion, Ekphonetheis en te aute Schole epi tou Hierodidaskalou Kyriou Athanasiou tou Pariou* ("Discourse of Praise, or Enco-

mium to Culture-loving Chios, Delivered in the School of Chios when the Priest-Teacher Athanasios Parios was Its Director"). Published in George I. Zolotas' *History of Chios*, Vol. 3^1, pp. 553-566.

(3) *Enkomion eis ten Auten, Ekphonethen eis to Scholeion tou Merikodidaskalou Kyriou Niketa Kontaratou 1802* ("Encomium to the Same, Delivered at the School of the Special Teacher Niketas Kontaratos in 1802"). Published in Zolotas' *History of Chios*, Vol. 3^1, pp. 567-575.

LIVES OF SAINTS

(1) *Bios kai Martyrion tou Hagiou Neomartyros Nikolaou tou Chiou* ("The Life and Martyrdom of the Holy Martyr Nicholas the Chian"). Published in the *New Martyrologion* of Sts. Macarios of Corinth and Nicodemos the Hagiorite, Venice, 1799; Athens, 1856, 1961. It has appeared also in the *New Chian Leimonarion* and the *Great Synaxaristes* of Victor Matthaiou, Vol. 10 (October).

(2) *Bios kai Politeia ton Hosion kai Theophoron Pateron hemon Niketa, Ioannou kai Ioseph, ton en Chio Askesanton* ("The Life and Conduct

of Our Holy and God-inspired Fathers Niketas, John and Joseph, Who Led a Life of Spiritual Endeavor in Chios"). Contained in the *Akoluthia* in honor of them that was published in 1804 at Venice, and is listed above under 'Books.' Reprinted in *Ta Neamonesia*, Book I, Chios, 1865, with many changes in the diction.

(3) *Bios tes Hagias Endoxou Parthenomartyros Myropes tes en Chio Athlesases* ("The Life of the Holy and Glorious Virgin-Martyr Myrope, Who Suffered Martyrdom in Chios"). Published in the *New Leimonarion* and the *New Chian Leimonarion*.

(4) *Bios tou Hagiou Demetriou tou Peloponnesiou* ("The Life of Saint Demetrios the Peloponnesian"). Published in the *New Leimonarion*.

(5) *Bios tou Hagiou Hosiomartyros Louka tou Neou* ("The Life of the Holy Hosiomartyr Luke the New"). Published in the *New Leimonarion* and the *Great Synaxaristes* of Constantine Doukakis, Vol. 7 (March).

(6) *Bios tou Hagiou Martyros Theophilou* ("The Life of the Holy Martyr Theophilos"). Published in the *New Leimonarion,* the *New*

Chian Leimonarion, and the *Great Synaxaristes* of Doukakis, Vol. 11 (July), and that of Matthaiou, Vol. 7 (July).

(7) *Bios tou Hagiou Neomartyros Ioannou tou ek Thessalonikes* ("The Life of the Holy Neomartyr John of Thessaloniki"). Published in the *New Leimonarion* and the *Great Synaxaristes* of Matthaiou, Vol. 5 (May).

(8) *Bios tou Hagiou Neomartyros Lazarou* ("The Life of the Holy Neomartyr Lazarus"). Published in the *New Leimonarion,* the *Great Synaxaristes* of Doukakis, Vol. 8 (April), and that of Matthaiou, Vol. 4 (April).

(9) *Martyrion tou Hagiou Endoxou kai Kallinikou Neomartyros Angele tou en Chio Athlesantos* ("The Martyrdom of the Holy, Glorious and Triumphant Neomartyr Angelis, Who Suffered Martyrdom in Chios"). Published in the *New Leimonarion,* the *New Chian Leimonarion,* and the *Great Synaxaristes* of Matthaiou, Vol. 12 (December).

(10) *Martyrion tou Hagiou Neomartyros Georgiou tou Chiopolitou* ("The Martyrdom of the Holy Neomartyr George of Chios"). Appeared in the *New Leimonarion* and the *New Chian Lei-*

monarion. It has also been published separately at Hermoupolis, Syros, in 1848.

(11) *Bios kai Martyrion tes Hagias Parthenomartyros kai Athlophorou tou Christou Markelles tes ek tes Nesou Chiou* ("The Life and Martyrdom of the Holy Virgin-Martyr and Victor of Christ Markella of the Island of Chios"). Corrected by St. Nikephoros. Published in the *New Leimonarion,* the *New Chian Leimonarion,* and the *Great Synaxaristes* of Doukakis, Vol. 11 (July).

(12) *Bios tes Hosias Metros hemon Matrones tes Thaumatourgou* ("The Life of Our Holy Mother Matrona the Miracle-worker"). Written by another writer and corrected in diction and composition by St. Nikephoros. Published in the *New Leimonarion,* the *New Chian Leimonarion,* and the *Great Synaxaristes* of Matthaiou, Vol. 10 (October).

HYMNOGRAPHICAL WORKS

1. *Akoluthias*

(1) *Akolouthia tou Hagiou Endoxou Neomartyros Nikolaou tou Chiou* ("Akoluthia of the Holy Neomartyr Nicholas of Chios"). Published in the *New Martyrologion* by Sts. Macarios of

Corinth and Nicodemos the Hagiorite, and in the *New Chian Leimonarion.*

(2) *He Theia kai Hiera Akolouthia ton Hosion kai Theophoron Pateron Hemon Niketa, Ioannou, kai Ioseph* ("The Divine and Holy Akoluthia of Our Holy and God-inspired Fathers Niketas, John and Joseph"). Published as part of Nikephoros' book that contains a history and description of Nea Moni (Venice, 1804), in *Ta Neamonesia,* Book I, Chios, 1865, in the 4th ed. of the *New Leimonarion,* and in the *New Chian Leimonarion.*

(3) *Akolouthia tes Hagias Megalomartyros Myropes* ("Akoluthia of the Holy Great Martyr Myrope"). Published in the *New Leimonarion* and the *New Chian Leimonarion.*

(4) *Akolouthia tou Hagiou Demetriou tou Peloponnesiou* ("Akoluthia of Saint Demetrios the Peloponnesian"). Published in the *New Leimonarion.*

(5) *Akolouthia tou Hagiou Endoxou Neomartyros Georgiou tou Chiou* ("Akoluthia of the Holy and Glorious Neomartyr George the Chian"). Published in the *New Leimonarion* and the *New Chian Leimonarion.*

(6) *Akolouthia tou Hagiou Martyros Theophilou* ("Akoluthia of the Holy Martyr Theophilos"). Published in the *New Leimonarion* and the *New Chian Leimonarion;* separately in 1856, in Zakynthos (Zante) ; and together with the akoluthia of this saint written by George Koressios, in 1883, at Athens.

(7) *Akolouthia tou Hagiou Megalomartyros Markou tou Neou* ("Akoluthia of the Holy Megalomartyr Mark the New"). Published in the *New Leimonarion* and the *New Chian Leimonarion.*

(8) *Akolouthia tou Hagiou Neomartyros Angele* ("Akoluthia of the Holy Neomartyr Angelis"). Published in the *New Leimonarion* and the *New Chian Leimonarion.*

(9) *Akolouthia tou Hagiou Endoxou Neomartyros Georgiou, Hostis Emartyresen en te Nea Epheso* ("Akolouthia of the Holy and Glorious Neomartyr George, Who Suffered Martyrdom in New Ephesus"). Published in the *New Leimonarion.*

(10) *Akolouthia tou Hagiou Neomartyros Lazarou* ("Akoluthia of the Holy Neomartyr Lazarus"). Published in the *New Leimonarion.*

(11) *Akolouthia tou Hagiou Hosiomartyros*

Louka tou Neou ("Akoluthia of the Holy Hosio-martyr Luke the New"). Published in the *New Leimonarion.*

(12) *Akolouthia tou en Hagiois Patros hemon Makariou Archiepiskopou Korinthou tou Notara* ("Akoluthia of Our Father among Saints Maca-rios Notaras, Archbishop of Corinth"). Pub-lished in 1863, in Chios; in 1885, at Hermoupolis; some years later, at Athens in Doukakis' *Great Synaxaristes;* and also in the 4th ed. of the *New Leimonarion* and in the *New Chian Leimonarion.*

(13) *Akolouthia eis ten Heorten tes Heureseos tes Timias Karas tes Hosias Metros hemon Ma-trones tes Chiopolitidos* ("Akoluthia for the Feast of the Discovery of the Venerable Head of Our Holy Mother Matrona of Chios"). A corrected version of an older akoluthia. Published in the *New Leimonarion* and the *New Chian Leimo-narion.*

(14) *Akolouthia tes Hagias Parthenomartyros Markelles tes ek tes Nesou Chiou* ("Akoluthia of the Holy Virgin-Martyr Markella of the Island of Chios"). A corrected version of an older akolu-thia. Published in the *New Leimonarion* and the *New Chian Leimonarion,* and in pamphlet form in 1908 at Hermoupolis.

(15) *Akolouthia tou Hosiou kai Theophorou Patros hemon Gerasimou tou Neou* ("Akoluthia of Our Holy and God-inspired Father Gerasimos the New"). A corrected version of an older akoluthia. Published in the *New Leimonarion.*

2. Oikoi

Oikoi Eikosi Tessares eis ten Hosian kai Theophoron Metera hemon Matronan ten Chiopolitida ("Twenty-four Oikoi in Honor of Our Holy and God-inspired Mother Matrona of Chios"). Published in the *New Leimonarion* and the *New Chian Leimonarion.*

3. Other Hymnographical Works

(1) Three *prosomoia* in the akoluthia in honor of the martyr Polydoros, contained in the *New Leimonarion* and the *New Chian Leimonarion.*

(2) A *kontakion* in the preceding akoluthia.

(3) An *idiomelon* and a *doxastikon* in the akoluthia in honor of the martyr Phanourios contained in the *New Leimonarion* and the *New Chian Leimonarion.*

(4) Six *idiomela* in the akoluthia in honor of the Theotokos contained in the book: *Akolouthia*

tes Zoodochou Peges kai he kata to Genethleon tes Theotokou ("Akoluthia of the Source of Life and that of the Birth of the Theotokos"), ed. by K. Methodios, Chios, 1862, and in *Ta Neamonesia*, Chios, 1865.

SELECTED PASSAGES FROM THE PROSE WORKS OF THE SAINT

God-centeredness

Fortunate is the man who has come to have God as his helper and to have his hopes in Him alone. Let the Devil bear malice towards him, let all men persecute him and plot against him, let all his adversaries fight against him — he never fears anyone, because he has God as his helper. He remains always a victor, always glorified, always happy, always rich, always cheerful and joyful, even if he happens to fall into extreme poverty and into a great many adverse and grievous circumstances of the present life. For inasmuch as he hopes in Almighty God, he does not despair, he is not sorry, is not anxious, but expects help from Above. Fortunate, then, is such a man and worthy to be deemed happy, just as the Prophet-king David regards such a man as happy, saying:

"Blessed is he whose helper is the God of Jacob, whose hope is in the Lord his God."[1] Such were all the Prophets, the Apostles, the Martyrs, the Holy Ascetics and all the Saints from the beginning of time.[2]

* * *

To those who love God, everything is conducive to their good.[3]

* * *

The divine churches are works and signs of love for God.[4]

* * *

The Prophet-king David says[5] to God: "O Lord, I have loved the beauty of Thy house and the place of the tabernacle of Thy glory."[6]

Wisdom

Earthly wisdom (*epigeios sophia*) must be conjoined with heavenly wisdom (*ouranios sophia*). Or, to speak more aptly, heavenly wisdom, which is reverence for God (*theosebeia*), must be the starting point and foundation of education, for "the fear of the Lord is the beginning of wisdom."[7]

* * *

A distinguishing characteristic of every man

who possesses the virtue of moral wisdom (*phronesis*) is to take care not only for his own good, but also for the good of others.[8]

Holy Ascetics

The holy ascetics renounced all worldly things. They disciplined themselves, struggled persistently and diligently. Alone, they adhered firmly to God alone, through self-control, psalmody and prayer. Despising everything earthly and transitory, they had regard only for the heavenly and eternal. The thrice blessed ones aspired to achieve only one thing: to cleanse their soul of every worldly desire, to train themselves in the great and lofty virtues.[9]

Martyrs

The martyrs are heavenly wealth, a spiritual treasure, God-given saviors, helpers and public benefactors.[10]

* * *

Christ is the strength and power of martyrs.[11]

Martyrdom

Martyrdom is a Baptism done with blood, as Gregory the Theologian says; and hence he who is

baptized through martyrdom is not in fear of being defiled by new stains of sin. And as the holy
Clement, the author of the *Stromateis,* says, martyrdom is a purification from sins that is accompanied by glory. Thus, martyrdom is good, and
much better and more glorious than simple re-
pentance.[12]

* * *

According to our divine Fathers, martyrdom is
not simply absolution from sins, but is also sainthood, heavenly glory and honor.[13]

Honoring Saints

Although God's saints have no need of glory and
honor from men, since they enjoy heavenly and
divine glory, living in eternity according to Solomon, and their souls are in the hand of God, and
their names are recorded in the book of life,
nevertheless it is our indispensable duty to write
their lives and achievements for their glorification
and honor, and consequently to praise them and
pronounce them blessed, as faithful servants of
God, or rather as genuine friends of His. For
according to Basil the Great, the honor that is
given to the best of fellow-servants is proof of
goodwill towards our common Lord. This is especially true if these good servants of God are not

simply saints, if they did not simply struggle for their own Salvation, but were also public benefactors, who struggled for the salvation of many, and made myriads of efforts towards this end.[14]

Such were our Holy and God-inspired Fathers Niketas, John, and Joseph [founders of Nea Moni]. For they struggled not only for their own Salvation, but after their super-human efforts of spiritual endeavor over a period of many years they concerned themselves with the Salvation of the many. To this end these Fathers of blessed memory subjected themselves to myriads of pains, both on land and on sea, in their effort to build Monasteries for men's spiritual Salvation, and did actually build them. And through the divine example of their virtues and their God-inspired teaching they saved many. Wherefore, it is just that they be praised as our common benefactors, for the glory of God, Who is glorified in His Saints, and for the benefit of those who read or hear about their divine Conduct and their godlike virtues.

ANTHOLOGY FROM THE POETRY OF THE SAINT

(I have placed a heading over each group of troparia, to call attention to their dominant theme.)

Christ

Glory to Thy goodness, O Son and Logos of God, O transcendently good Jesus, for Thou didst not desire that the creature of Thine immaculate hands should perish, O lover of man; but through Thy good will and grace Thou didst lead Angelis, who denied Thee, from the fall of denial unto realization.[1]

* * *

O Christ, the strength of martyrs, Who didst strengthen also the new martyr Nicholas to contend in behalf of Thy divine name, by his intercessions grant us Thy great mercy.[2]

81

Who will not acclaim thee, O prize-winner of
the Lord, Nicholas, who will not praise thy glorious testimony? For thou didst clearly proclaim the
Logos of God, Who was born of the Father before
all ages, and in these later times assumed the nature of man; and thou didst boldly revile the
prime author of error as a deceiver and inventor
of every form of lawlessness. Wherefore, thou
didst cry out: I revere Christ, I worship Christ, I
renounce everything that I might gain Christ. But
now that thou standest before Him with the boldness of an athlete, intercede unceasingly with Him
for the sake of those who with faith and longing
celebrate thine ever-venerable memory.[3]

The Theotokos

Thou didst appear of old as a heavenly ladder
to Jacob our forefather, whereby minds ascend
from earth to the contemplation (*theoria*) of God,
worshipping with love thine ineffable offspring.[4]

*   *   *

Thou didst give birth to Him Who is by nature the Creator, and Who truly deified us
through the union that is above understanding,
O Theotokos, who art praised by all; Him do

thou entreat at length to illuminate us who praise thee in hymns.[5]

* * *

Having the pure beauty of thy soul most resplendent, O chaste Theotokos, and being filled from Heaven with the grace of God, thou dost ever shine with eternal light upon those who with joy cry out: Truly thou art above all, O pure Theotokos.[6]

Faith

The divine faith, O Angelis, which thou didst once abjure, thou didst regain, O blessed one, and straightway didst proclaim it before the godless tyrants; and having been slain, thou didst confirm it with thy blood, O prize-winner.[7]

* * *

Thou didst strive lawfully, O victorious one, and didst keep the faith in the Creator; therefore there is laid up for thee the crown of victory, O namesake of the angels.[8]

* * *

Great are the achievements of faith; in the flames of the fire, the holy martyr Theophilos rejoiced as if he were refreshed in water, and he loudly proclaimed Christ alone as God; and with

Him he intercedeth unceasingly that our souls be saved.[9]

Courage

Seeing thy courage, O glorious George, all the multitudes of angels rejoiced on high, and on earth below the Christian community of Kydoniai applauded thee.[10]

* * *

O how great was thy courage and fortitude, O martyr Nicholas! whereby, O all-praiseworthy one, having endured the fearful struggles of martyrdom, thou didst proclaim Christ before the tyrants, and by thy words didst put to shame the descendants of Hagar, censuring them with divine boldness; wherefore we chant praises unto thee.[11]

* * *

Thou didst manifest invincible courage and unyielding endurance in tortures, O martyr Theophilos, and supernal and awesome fortitude while being burned in the fire, for which thou standest now before God rejoicing.[12]

Renunciation

Having estranged yourselves from earthly things, O heavenly-minded Niketas, John and Joseph, and having wisely renounced the pleasures of this life, ye became, O holy Fathers, intimates of God through purity of life.[13]

*   *   *

Ye renounced the world and the things of the world, O Fathers of blessed memory, and took upon your shoulders the cross, the good yoke of Christ our protector, and thus found divine rest of the soul.[14]

*   *   *

Wisely didst thou renounce the earth and consider all earthly things as rubbish, and having longed for things heavenly, O all-blessed Mark, thou didst exchange things fleeting for things abiding and eternal.[15]

Prayer

By ever devoting thyself to prayer, continence and inner wakefulness *(nepsis)*, O holy Myrope, thou didst mortify all the ungovernable assaults of the passions and didst become a sweet fragrance *(myron)* of Christ by the purity of thy life.[16]

*   *   *

As one anointed with the divine chrism of episcopacy, O Father Macarios, thou didst tend in a holy manner the divine flock of Christ that was entrusted unto thee. Then, by the toils of divine asceticism, thou didst wholly soar on high to divine love, O my fellow-spiritual striver of blessed memory, and even while living in the world, forthwith thou didst wholly become as it were a citizen of Heaven. Thou didst have thy spirit raised above the earth through mental prayer (*noera euche*) to the Lord, Whom do thou entreat to save and illuminate our souls.[17]

* * *

Let us honor by praise the divine hierarch and holy ascetic, the truly blessed Macarios, the archbishop of Corinth who was raised in the Peloponnesos, and became the divine guide of Chios. Let us chant to him melodiously: Rejoice, O sublime one, who by asceticism hast made resplendent the office of a hierarch. Rejoice, thou who didst mortify the passions by earnest continence, and through all-night standing, unceasing prayers and tears didst establish Christ in thy soul. Do thou entreat Him for the peace of the world and the salvation of our souls.[18]

Purification

Divinely purified in soul by means of spiritual practices, ye shone forth with the rays of the virtues, O Fathers of blessed memory (Niketas, John and Joseph), who are equal in number to the Trinity. And foreknowing by Divine inspiration things to come, O divine ones, ye declared them to Emperor Monomachos in Lesvos, and your prophecy was accomplished in deed.[19] ,

* * *

By godly acts and works thou didst purify thyself of every defilement of the flesh and spirit, ever occupying thyself with higher contemplations and directing all thine aspiration from earth to Heaven. Wherefore, O Myrope, thou didst in no wise spare thy temporary life, but didst prefer a voluntary death.[20]

Freedom from Passions

Leading a truly angelic life on earth, O holy Fathers Joseph, Niketas and John, ye peers of the angels and boast of the ascetics, ye acquired freedom from passions (*apatheia*) and rose swiftly to the divine height of the virtues, and now ye are united with the angels.[21]

* * *

Having first utterly dried up the slime of the passions through the hardships of spiritual endeavor (*askesis*) and the purification of dispassion

(*apatheia*), O divine Fathers, and having been
wholly purified and become radiant in mind by
the effulgences of the virtues, ye received of God,
O God-inspired ones, the knowledge of things to
come.[22]

* * *

In the stead of the prison and privation from
food to which thou wast subjected, the food of
Paradise hath been granted unto thee; and in the
stead of being shut up with horses, life with the
angels, O great martyr Nicholas. Wherefore, entreat Christ God to deliver us from the darkness
and irrationality of the passions, and to deem us,
who with longing celebrate thy memory, worthy
of passing the remainder of our life in works of
light and the repose of freedom from passions.[23]

Chastity

Having lived in chastity and holiness, with
continence, inner wakefulness and attention, and
having adorned thyself with every form of virtue,
thou didst become a spotless bride of Christ, O
all-blessed Matrona.[24]

Love

The heavenly fire was lit in thee, O athlete of
Christ, the same which the Lord came to send on

earth, O blessed Angelis, and it set aflame thy heart with divine love.[25]

Possessing the immaterial flame in thy heart, O Theophilos, thrice-blessed victorious one of the Lord, thou didst undergo the burning of the material flame; and while burning therein thou didst cry out: Now I surrender my spirit into Thy hands, O Christ, Thou strength of the martyrs.[26]

* * *

Thou didst raise thy mind above things visible, O godly-minded Theophilos; wherefore nothing separated thee from thy divine love for Christ — neither prison, nor fire, O thou of all-blessed memory.[27]

Theosis

That He might deify man, O pure Theotokos, God through thee became man, Whom the renowned and victorious George of Chios glorified, and he proclaimed thee to be a virgin mother.[28]

* * *

The Lord tested thee like gold in the furnace of tortures while on earth, O Nicholas, and having received thee as a divine burnt-offering, He made thee a partaker of Divine glory.[29]

Having lived blamelessly and completed thy
life in martyrdom, O all-praiseworthy Myrope,
thou didst receive from God the deserved crown
of incorruption. And now as thou standest together with the martyrs before the Divine throne,
and by participation dost behold the chosen ones
since the world began, and as one filled with the
glory and splendor that flasheth forth thence, re-
member us also who with faith and love celebrate
thine ever-venerable memory.[30]

The Immortal Life

Chanting in the Spirit, the most divine David
said that the death of the saints is precious (ti-
mios) in the sight of the Lord;[31] and the most wise
one saith that "the souls of the righteous are in the
hand of God Who saveth, and no torment shall
touch them."[32]

*　*　*

When ye finished the course of holy askesis
without going astray, O God-inspired Fathers,[33] ye
arrived at the divine habitations and took up your
dwelling with all the companies of the saints. And
having become partakers of the unending and
wholly inexpressible bliss, ye rejoice, O blessed
ones, in the presence of God.[34]

NOTES

INTRODUCTORY

[1] *Neohellenike Philologia* ("Modern Greek Literature"), Athens, 1868, p. 510.

[2] *Hagiologion tes Orthodoxou Ekklesias*, Athens, 1960, p. 355.

[3] *Historia tes Chiou*, Vol. 3^1, Athens, 1926, p. 502.

[4] *Ibid.*, pp. 523, 534, 537, 550.

[5] Regarding the Kollyvades Movement, see my book *St. Macarios of Corinth* (*Modern Orthodox Saints*, Vol. 2), 1972, pp. 15-31.

[6] *Op. cit.*, pp. 523, 551; Vol. 3^2, Athens, 1928, p. 57.

[7] *Op. cit.*, Vol. 3^1, pp. 523.

[8] First edition, Venice, 1819.

[9] Zolotas, *op. cit.*, Vol. 3^1, p. 573.

[10] *Ibid.*, p. 567.

[11] *Ibid.*, p. 568.

[12] That is, in the island of Chios.

[13] Zolotas, *op. cit.*, Vol. 3¹, p. 568.

[14] *Ibid.*, p. 565.

[15] *Ibid.*

[16] *Ibid.*, p. 568.

[17] *Ibid.*, p. 572.

[18] *Ibid.*

[19] *Ibid.*, pp. 571-572.

[20] *Rhetorike Techne.*

[21] *Rhetorike Pragmateia.*

[22] Constantine Cavarnos, *Modern Orthodox Saints*, Vol. 1, *St. Cosmas Aitolos*, 1971, 1975, p. 27.

[23] Zolotas, *op. cit.*, Vol. 3¹, p. 531.

[24] *Ibid.*, pp. 570-571.

[25] *Ibid.*, pp. 575-576.

[26] *Ibid.*, p. 555.

[27] *Ibid.*, pp. 555, 569, 572.

[28] *Ibid.*, p. 550.

[29] The Turks caused extensive destruction to Nea Moni in 1822. See note 14 in the section that follows. In 1881, there was a dreadful earthquake that caused further destruction to it.

[30] Zolotas, *op. cit.*, Vol. 3¹, p. 533.

[31] *Ibid.*, p. 523.

[32] Augustinos Kantiotis, ed., *Ho Hagios Kosmas ho Aitolos* ("Saint Cosmas Aitolos"), Athens, 1959, p. 337.

[33] *Neon Chiakon Leimonarion* ("New Chian Leimonarion"), Athens, 1968, p. 199. Henceforth I shall refer to this book as *NCL*.

[34] Zolotas, *op. cit.*, Vol. 3[1], p. 561.

[35] Byzantine music has eight Modes: four 'chief' or 'authentic' and four 'plagal.'

[36] *Aleiptes* means 'anointer.' It was used by the ancients to denote also a 'trainer' in gymnasia. The Greek Church writers early adopted the term *aleiptes* and the verb *aleiphein* or *epaleiphein* in a metaphorical sense in speaking of those who prepared their fellow Christians for the contest of martyrdom. Thus, St. Athanasios (*c.* 296-373) says that St. Antony the Great exerted himself very zealously *epaleiphein,* 'to train,' the holy martyrs at Alexandria (Migne, *Patrologia Graeca,* Vol. 26 col. 909).

[37] Matthew 10: 33.

[38] *NCL,* p. 167; Zolotas, *op. cit.,* Vol. 3[1], p. 525.

[39] *NCL,* pp. 200-201, 238-239.

[40] Zolotas, *op. cit.,* Vol. 3[2], p. 90.

[41] *Ibid.,* Vol. 3[2], p. 87.

[42] *NCL,* p. 113; Zolotas, *op. cit.,* Vol. 3[1], p. 566.

[43] Cf. Zolotas, *op. cit.,* Vol. 3[1], p. 552.

[44] *NCL,* p. 202.

[45] Bishop's chief assistant.

[46] *NCL,* pp. 195, 196.

[47] *Threskeutike kai Ethike Enkyklopaideia,* Vol. 9, Athens, 1966, p. 494.

[48] See pp. 9, 95, 96, 201, 269, 279, 284, 352, 359.

THE LIFE OF SAINT NIKEPHOROS
By Emily Sarou

[1] The text that follows is a somewhat abridged transla-

tion of *Bios tou Hosiou Nikephorou tou Chiou*, "The Life of Saint Nikephoros of Chios," contained in *NCL*, pp. 199-203.

[2] The name is spelled differently by other writers. Thus, Ioannes M. Andreadis spells it Giorgos (*Historia tes en Chio Ekklesias*, "History of the Church in Chios," Pt. I, Athens, 1940, p. 161), while Constantine I. Amantos spells it Georgos (*Ta Grammata eis ten Chion kata ten Tourkokratian*, "Learning in Chios During the Period of Turkish Rule," Piraeus, 1946, p. 158).

[3] Neither Emily Sarou nor her father, George Zolotas, from whose manuscripts she drew her information, tells us the year when the Saint began to teach, or the school or schools, other than the chief school of the island, where he taught. From Amantos, we learn that besides this School, there was one at the Monastery of Minas and one at Mastichochora, probably in the village of Harmoleia (*op. cit.*, pp. 16-17). But it is not likely that he taught at these, as there is no indication in the biography or in Zolotas' *History of Chios* that St. Nikephoros ever dwelt either at the Monastery of Minas or at Mastichochora. We may assume, then, that he commenced his career as a teacher at some elementary school in the city of Chios as well as at the main school of this city.

[4] The monastery was set on fire by the Turks twice in 1822, and again in 1828. See Andreas Styl. Axiotakis, *He Nea Mone tes Chiou* ("Nea Moni of Chios"), Chios, 1969, pp. 31-32, and note 14 below.

[5] Joseph, a native of Fourna, in Agrapha, Thessaly, had taught at the School of Chios (Zolotas, *History of Chios*, Vol. 3^1, p. 551; Eustratiadis, *Hagiology of the Orthodox Church*, p. 353).

[6] New Ephesus, in Asia Minor.

[7] Parios died in 1813.

[8] E.g. by Adamantios Korais (1748-1833) and Constantine Koumas (1777-1836).

[9] St. Macarios of Corinth is not mentioned, because he died years earlier, in 1805.

[10] Sarou mentions next Mark the New. I have omitted him, because his life was actually written by Athanasios Parios. See *NCL*, p. 237, and Eustratiadis, *op. cit.*, p. 304.

[11] The house of his sister.

[12] In 1845. See Zolotas, *op. cit.*, 3^1, p. 552.

[13] The biographer does not name the church. I have added its name to her statement. See *NCL*, p. 203.

[14] That is, the devastation of Chios in 1822, during which most of the Greek population of the island were slaughtered or taken captives. George Finlay (1799-1875), who has written a seven-volume history of Greece, has given a detailed account of it in the sixth volume of this work. I shall only quote what he says happened at two monasteries: Aghios Minas and Nea Moni: "Three thousand Chiots retired to the monastery of Aghios Minas, five miles to the southward of the city. . . . The Turks surrounded the building and summoned them to surrender. The men had little hope of escaping death. The women and children were sure of being sold as slaves. Though they had no military leader, and were unable to take effectual measures for defending the monastery, they refused to lay down their arms. The Turks carried the building by storm, and put all within to the sword. Two thousand persons had also sought an asylum in the fine old monastery of Nea Moni, which is about six miles from the city, secluded in the mountains towards the west. . . . The Turks stormed this monastery as they had done that of Aghios Minas. A number of the helpless inmates had shut themselves up in the church. The doors were forced open, and the Turks, after slaughtering even the women on their knees at prayer, set fire to the screen of paintings in the church, and to the wood-work and roofs of the other buildings in the monastery, and left the Christians who were not already slain to perish in the conflagration." (*A History of Greece*, Vol. 6, Oxford, 1877, pp. 255-256.) Francois Pouqueville (1770-1838) says that the number of *monks* who were

massacred at Nea Moni was two hundred (*Histoire de la regeneration de la Grece,* Paris, 1825, 2nd ed., Vol. 3, pp. 479-481).

[15] That is, in 1822, when both suffered martyrdom at the hands of the Turks.

[16] Sarou says simply "teacher of music" (*mousikodidaskalos*). I have interpreted this to mean teacher of *church* music, both because that was the only music St. Nikephoros was skilled in, and also because I cannot conceive of a disciple of the Saint occupying himself with secular music.

SELECTED PASSAGES FROM
THE PROSE WORKS OF THE SAINT

[1] Psalm 145: 5 (Septuagint).

[2] *NCL,* p. 300.

[3] *Logos Enkomiastikos e Enkomion pros ten Philomouson Chion,* in G. I. Zolotas, *The History of Chios,* Vol. 3[1], p. 559.

[4] *Ibid.,* p. 558.

[5] Psalm 25: 8 (Septuagint).

[6] *Logos Enkomiastikos,* p. 558.

[7] *Ibid.,* p. 565. The quotation is from Proverbs 1: 7.

[8] *Ibid.,* pp. 555-556.

[9] *NCL,* p. 225.

[10] *Logos Enkomiastikos,* p. 566.

[11] *Bios kai Martyrion tou Hagiou Nikolaou tou Chiou,* in *New Martyrologion,* Athens, 1961, pp. 166-167, and *NCL,* p. 58.

[12] *Martyrion tou Hagiou Demetriou tou Peloponnesiou,* in *New Leimonarion,* p. 133.

[13] *NCL,* p. 113.

[14] *NCL,* p. 225.

ANTHOLOGY FROM THE POETRY
OF THE SAINT

[1] *NCL,* p. 109.

[2] *NCL,* p. 53.

[3] *NCL,* p. 51.

[4] *NCL,* p. 236.

[5] *NCL,* p. 53.

[6] *NCL,* p. 118.

[7] *Ibid.*

[8] *NCL,* p. 117.

[9] *NCL,* p. 277.

[10] *NCL,* p. 98.

[11] *NCL,* p. 52.

[12] *NCL,* p. 279.

[13] *NCL,* p. 224.

[14] *NCL,* p. 222.

[15] *NCL,* p. 234.

[16] *NCL,* p. 105.

[17] *NCL,* p. 181.

[18] *NCL,* p. 178.

[19] *NCL,* p. 221.

[20] *NCL,* p. 104.

[21] *NCL,* p. 222.

[22] *NCL,* p. 223.

[23] *NCL,* p. 51.

[24] *NCL,* p. 308.

[25] *NCL,* p. 113.

[26] *NCL,* p. 278.

[27] *Ibid.*

[28] *NCL,* p. 98.

[29] *NCL,* p. 59.

[30] *NCL,* p. 103.

[31] Psalm 115: 6 (Septuagint).

[32] *NCL,* p. 230. The quotation is from *The Wisdom of Solomon* 3: 1.

[33] Niketas, John, and Joseph, founders of Nea Moni.

[34] *NCL,* p. 230.

APPENDIX

BRIEF BIOGRAPHIES
OF NEOMARTYRS AND OTHER
ORTHODOX SAINTS TREATED IN
ST. NIKEPHOROS' WORKS AND
MENTIONED IN THIS BOOK

I am placing the saints in three groups: (1) Neomartyrs, (2) Older Martyrs, and (3) Holy Ascetics (*Hosioi*). For convenient reference, I have ordered the names alphabetically. In each biographical sketch I have given in parentheses the month and the day when the saint is commemorated. In the case of the neomartyrs, the date is that when they died.

1. *Neomartyrs*

ANGELIS, *who suffered martyrdom in 1813 in Chios* (December 3). — A native of Argos in the Peloponnesos, this neomartyr was a practical physician. He abjured his Christian faith, and espoused the religion of the Turks, Islam. Later he repented and went to Chios. Here, after being duly prepared for martyrdom by St. Nikephoros, he appeared before the Turkish authorities and declared that he was no longer a Turk, but a Christian. When the Turks saw that both flattery and threats failed utterly to change his resolution, they imprisoned him and afterward beheaded him.

DEMETRIOS OF CHIOS, *who was martyred in 1802 at Constantinople* (January 29). — Demetrios was born in Palaiokastron, Chios, of poor parents. At an early age, he went to Constantinople and secured employment. Here, denying his Christian faith, he embraced Islam. Soon, however, he repented his act, and appearing before the Turkish authorities declared that he was a Christian and was resolved to remain a Christian, regardless of their threats. This enraged the Turks. They seized him, beat him severely with rods, and finally beheaded him.

DEMETRIOS THE PELOPONNESIAN, *who suffered martyrdom in 1803 at Tripolis of the Peloponnesos* (April 14).—This neomartyr was a native of Ligouditsa in Arcadia. He became a servant of a Turkish family at Tripolis. Yielding to their continual incitement to espouse their religion, he renounced his Christian faith. But soon he began to have strong feelings of remorse for his act. So he went to a monastery, confessed to the abbot and sought his advice. The abbot sent him, with a letter of introduction, to St. Macarios of Corinth in Chios. Here he received very valuable spiritual training and guidance, both from St. Macarios and from St. Nikephoros. Duly prepared by them for martyrdom, Demetrios returned to Tripolis ready to profess his faith openly and to die for it. When the Turks at Tripolis saw him and heard him say that he was a Christian and was resolved to die a Christian, they seized him, subjected him to many kinds of tortures, and finally beheaded him.

GEORGE OF CHIOS, *who suffered martyrdom in 1807 in Kydoniai* (November 26) . — Born in the Chian village of Pityos, George became at a very early age an apprentice to a woodcarver. While occupied by the latter in the island of Psara, he ran away to the city of Kavalla, in northern Greece. He was ten years old then.

Having stolen some watermelons from a garden, he was caught by the owner and was taken to the judge, a Turk. Frightened, he denied his Christian faith and became a Moslem. After working for some time for Turks, he left Kavalla and went to Chios and thence to Kydoniai, a city on the west coast of Asia Minor. Here he repented for his act and returned to Christianity. When the Turks of Kydoniai learned, years later, that he had been for a time a Moslem and despised their religion, they became very angry. They arrested him and cast him into prison. Having tried him, they condemned him to death. They shot him from behind and then beheaded him.

GEORGE OF EPHESUS, *who suffered martyrdom in 1801 at Ephesus* (April 5) . — While in a state of intoxication, this neomartyr was induced to embrace Islam. Soon, however, he repented and returned to the Christian religion. When the Turks learned this, they seized him, cast him into prison, and here subjected him to all sorts of tortures. Having failed by these means to cause him to return to their faith, they beheaded him.

JOHN (OR NANNOS) OF THESSALONIKI, *who was martyred in 1802 at Smyrna* (May 29) .

— John was a leather-cutter, and worked with his father at Smyrna. He was very fond of reading the lives of martyrs, and there developed in him the desire to become himself a martyr. To this end, he feigned denial of his faith and the espousal of Islam. Some days later, he presented himself to the Turks as a despiser of their religion, and boldly professed his faith in Christ. This resulted in his being seized by the Turks, imprisoned, and then beheaded.

LAZARUS THE BULGAR, *who suffered martyrdom in 1802 at Pergamus* (April 23). — This native of Kamprova, in Bulgaria, worked as a shepherd in the region of Pergamus, in northwestern Asia Minor. Slandered by a Turkish woman, he was seized by the Turks and subjected to dreadful tortures, in order to force him to renounce his Christian faith and embrace their religion. As he steadfastly refused to do this, he was beheaded.

LUKE THE NEW, *who suffered martyrdom in 1802 in Mytilene* (March 23). — This saint is called an *hosiomartyr,* because he was both a holy ascetic and a martyr. He was born in Adrianople, Thrace. Orphaned at an early age, he sought and found employment in Mytilene, doing chores for a merchant. Here he quarreled with a Turkish youth and wounded him. Thereupon the Turks seized him and forced him to become a Moslem. Later, he came to realize the gravity of the sin he had thus committed, and fled from Mytilene to Mount Athos. He confessed his sin at the Skete of St. Anne, returned to Christianity, and became a monk. After a certain number of years on Athos, he visited Mytilene with his Elder, hieromonk Basil. Recognizing Luke, the Turks seized him, tortured him very cruelly, and finally beheaded him.

MARK THE NEW, *who suffered martyrdom in 1801 in Chios* (June 5). — A native of Smyrna, Mark was a traveling vendor at Kousantasi of Smyrna. Here he committed adultery, and the judge, a Turk, condemned him to death, but told him that he could escape death by becoming a Moslem. Thereupon, Mark abjured the Christian religion. But soon he began to have feelings of remose for his apostasy. Tormented by his conscience, he went to Trieste, then to Russia, then to Chios, next to New Ephesus, and finally again to Chios. In Chios he received counsel and inspiration from Sts. Macarios and Nikephoros. When he was duly prepared, he appeared before the Turkish judge and professed the Christian faith. This resulted in his being cast into prison, tortured, and beheaded.

NICHOLAS, *who suffered martyrdom in 1754 in Chios* (October 31). — This neomartyr was born in the village of Karyes in Chios. At the age of twenty, he went to Magnesia, Asia Minor, and worked as a mason. One day he woke up in a state of mental derangement. Although he did not perform any acts of madness, he was visibly in a state of confusion. Seeing him in this state, the Turks pressured him to become a Moslem. He yielded without great resistance. After this, his fellow-Chiots brought him back to Chios. Here, under the care and guidance of a pious priest, he recovered fully his sanity and returned to the Orthodox Christian faith. Having learned that he abjured their religion, the Turks in Chios were infuriated. They seized him and subjected him to dreadful tortures, in order to make him return to Islam. But meeting with failure, they beheaded him.

THEOPHILOS OF ZAKYNTHOS (ZANTE), *who was martyred in 1635 in Chios* (July 24).

— A native of the island of Zakynthos, Theophilos worked as a sailor in a ship whose captan was a Chian. Displeased by the captain, he left the ship upon their arrival in Chios. Here, a Turkish skipper sought to get Theophilos to work for him. But Theophilos refused. The skipper became very angry and told the Turks that Theophilos had worn a Turkish fez and hence ought to espouse their religion. As Theophilos steadfastly refused to do this, he was tortured, thrown into a fire and burned to death.

2. *Older Martyrs*

MARKELLA OF CHIOS (July 22). — It is not known when the martyr Markella lived. But what is said in some troparia in her akoluthia makes it clear that the author of the akoluthia believed that she flourished after the time of St. Matrona, i.e. some time after the middle of the fourteenth century. From long ago there existed a church in Chios dedicated to her, and she has been credited with many miracles. In her life contained in the *New Leimonarion,* she is presented as a native of the Chian village of Volissos. According to St. Nikephoros, she was killed by her father, because she would not yield to his lewd desires.

MYROPE, *who suffered martyrdom in Chios* (December 2). — Myrope was born and baptized in Ephesus, Asia Minor. During the reign of Decius (249-251), her mother took her to Chios, where they had an estate. It happened that at this time St. Isidore had been martyred in Chios. The pagan ruler of Chios, Numerius, issued an order that St. Isidore's body remain unburied, to be eaten by vultures. Disregarding this order, Myrope went at night, took the body of the martyr away, and buried it at a suitable place. When the absence of the body was reported to Numerius the next day, he threatened to put to death the soldiers who had been appointed to guard the body, if they failed to find it. Learning this, Myrope appeared before the ruler and declared fearlessly that she was the one who had taken away the body and buried it, because she despised his wretched atheism. Thereupon, enraged, Numerius ordered his soldiers to torture her and cast her into prison. She died in prison.

3. *Holy Ascetics*

GERASIMOS THE NEW, *who dwelt in Kephallenia* (October 20). — A native of Trikkala in the province of Corinth, Gerasimos was a descendant of the distinguished Byzantine house of Notaras. He visited various places in Zakynthos (Zante), and also Constantinople and its environs, the Holy Mountain of Athos and many monasteries of Anatolia, and finally Jerusalem. At Jerusalem, he served for a year as sacristan in the Church of the Resurrection. Then he was ordained here deacon and presbyter by Patriarch Germanos. Leaving Jerusalem, he visited Mount Sinai, Egypt, Crete, and finally Zakynthos, where he settled in a cave. Here, he led a life of askesis for about six years. Finally, he went to the island of Kephallenia (Cephalonia), built a convent for nuns, which he named New Jerusalem, and there continued his life of spiritual endeavor. He died in peace at this convent on August 15, 1579. St. Gerasimos is a very popular saint. His akoluthia has gone through at least nineteen editions.

MACARIOS NOTARAS, *Archbishop of Corinth* (April 17). — Macarios was born in Corinth in 1731, of the famous Notaras family. He was educated in Corinth, and taught here gratis for a number of years. Having distinguished himself as a teacher and gained the deep respect of the people of Corinth for his exemplary life, he was elected by them, clergy and laymen, to succeed Archbishop Parthenios of Corinth, who died in 1764. He was ordained their bishop in January of 1765 at Constantinople by Patriarch Samuel. When the Russo-Turkish war of 1768 broke out, he had to leave Corinth, together with his family. He went to Zakynthos and thence to the island of Hydra, where he lived in a monastery. When the war ended, the Holy Synod of the Ecumenical Patriarchate, under the pressure of the Turks, elected a new bishop for Corinth. As a result, Macarios did not return to his province, but visited various monastic centers, particularly Mount Athos and Patmos, and finally settled at a hermitage in Chios. He died in peace on April 17, 1805, at his hermitage in Chios. For a detailed account of his life, character, thought and publications see my book *St. Macarios of Corinth*, Vol. 3 of *Modern Orthodox Saints*.

MATRONA OF CHIOS (October 20). — Matrona was born in the village of Volissos in Chios, of pious and wealthy parents. She manifested monastic tendencies at an early age and, leaving her parents, she went to a solitary region, where she built a small convent. Gradu-

ally, other nuns joined her, and they led together a life of spiritual endeavor. Having distinguished herself for her holy way of life, and
performed many miracles in her lifetime and
after her repose, she has been greatly revered
in Chios. She died some time in the 14th century.

NIKETAS, JOHN, AND JOSEPH, *founders of
the monastery Nea Moni in Chios* (May 20). —
These saints, natives of Chios, first led a life of
spiritual endeavor in a cave on the mountain
Provateion of this island. Having found a
miracle-working icon of the Theotokos sus-
pended on a myrtle, they erected at the site a
chapel in honor of the Theotokos and dwelt
nearby. Later, with the help provided by the
Byzantine Emperor Constantine Monomachos
(1042-1054), whose rise to the imperial throne
they had foretold him, they built *Nea Moni,*
'the New Monastery,' and its magnificent church
dedicated to the Theotokos. Here they continued their godly life of spiritual striving and
died in peace.

SELECTED BIBLIOGRAPHY

Akolouthia tou en Hagiois Patros hemon Makariou Archiepiskopou Korinthou tou Notara ("Akoluthia of Our Father among Saints Macarios Notaras, Archbishop of Corinth"), by Athanasios Parios and St. Nikephoros of Chios, edited by the hieromonk Joseph the Chian. Chios, 1863.

Akolouthia tou Hosiou Nikephorou tou Chiou hypo tou Protosyngellou Kyrillou Trehake, kai Bios Autou hypo A.G.Z. ("Akoluthia of Saint Nikephoros of Chios by the Protosyngellos Kyrillos Trehakis, and His Life by A.G.Z. i.e. Aimilia George Zolota, later Aimilia or or 'Emily' Sarou. Chios, 1907; 2nd ed., in the *New Chian Leimonarion*.

Amantos, Constantine I., *Ta Grammata eis ten*

Chion kata ten Tourkokratian — *1566-1822* ("Learning in Chios During the Period of Turkish Rule — 1566-1822"). Piraeus, 1946.

Argenti, Philip P., *Bibliography of Chios, from Classical Times to 1936.* Oxford, 1940.

Doukakis, Constantine, *Megas Synaxaristes* ("Great Collection of Lives of Saints"). Athens, 1889-1896.

Eustratiadis, Sophronios, *Hagiologion tes Orthodoxou Ekklesias* ("Hagiology of the Orthodox Church"). Athens, 1960.

Matthaiou, Victor, *Ho Megas Synaxaristes tes Orthodoxou Ekklesias* ("The Great Collection of Lives of Saints of the Orthodox Church"). Athens, 1946-1950, and later editions.

Neon Chiakon Leimonarion ("New Chian Leimonarion"), 2nd edition, enlarged and improved by Christophoros K. Gerazounis. Athens, 1968.

Neon Leimonarion ("New Leimonarion" — i.e. Spiritual Meadows), by St. Macarios of Corinth, Athanasios Parios, and St. Nikephoros of Chios. Venice, 1819.

Nicodemos the Hagiorite, *Neon Martyrologion* ("New Martyrologion"). 3rd edition, Athens, 1961.

Papadopoulos, Chrysostomos, *Hoi Neomartyres* ("The Neomartyrs"). 3rd ed., Athens, 1970.

Petit, Louis, *Bibliographie des acolouthies grecques*. Bruxelles, 1926.

Sathas, Constantine N., *Neohellenike Philologia* ("Modern Greek Literature"). Athens, 1863.

Ta Neamonesia, Dyo Biblia, hon to men A' Ekdothen to 1804 hypo tou Hierodidaskalou Nikephorou, to de B' Synthachthen hypo tou Kathegoumenou Gregoriou Photeinou, Synexedothe meta tou A' Diorthothentos hypo tou Autou ("Writings Pertaining to Nea Moni, of Which the First was Published in 1804 by the Priest-Teacher Nikephoros, While the Second was Written by Abbot Gregory Photinos and was Published Together with the First after the Latter had been Corrected by Him"). Chios, 1865. The 'corrections' of Gregory Photinos consisted in translating St. Nikephoros' book from the vernacular of his time to older Greek diction.

Vretos, Andreas Papadopoulos, *Neohellenike Phi-*

lologia ("Modern Greek Literature"). Part I,
Athens, 1854.

Zolotas, George I., *Historia tes Chiou* ("The History of Chios"). Vol. 1^1, Athens, 1921; Vol. 2,
1924; Vol. 3^1, 1926; Vol. 3^2, 1928.

INDEX

115